A Free-Range Human
in a *Caged World*

From Primalization
into Civilization

Roger Gilbertson

To my Friend! Leslie!

A Finagle Watcher Book

First Edition

Published in the United States of America

ISBN   978-0-9859858-0-6   mBook
ISBN   978-0-9859858-1-3   eBook

Roger Gilbertson
Box 103
Washington, DC
20044-0103

http://www.RogerGilbertson.com

First Edition: November 2012

A Finagle Watcher Book

1 3 5 7 9 10 8 6 4 2

Gilbertson, Roger, 1936-

A Free-Range Human In A Caged World / Roger Gilbertson

"Roger, you are a philosopher-prince!"
U.S. Senator Max Cleland

"Your gathering hunting band metaphors give me a better understanding of what it means to be civilized."
Dr. Ron Smith, Psychiatrist

"I learned a lot and very much enjoyed your book.
I could hear your voice throughout."
Tefft Smith, Esquire

"Thank you for getting our retreat
started with stories that penetrate into the mind!"
Wyman Howard, Retreat Leader

"Thanks for giving me a working knowledge
of how ancient wisdom can be used today."
Tom Ward

"I have written 1,500 speeches.
You just gave the best speech I've ever heard!"
A Professional Speech Writer

Roger Gilbertson

Brief Contents

Figure Index

How did my Mother get me started

on an adventure in life learning?

Do your speculations

resonate with mine?

Full Contents

Thanks, Mom!

Myrtle Julianna Gunderson Gilbertson – thank you for all you gave me! A start in life, free as a child of Primalization! Yet we were imbedded in Civilization.

You gave me the gift of learning how to learn, by playing. Always fun to know more! To love learning!

Seven years of home un-schooling. You knew how children developed. You had many years of one-room school house mentoring, the vertical column of students who also teach.

I started the first grade in the regular, formal, "school factory" with an already activated, inspired lust for learning. A love of idea searching. Finding many views on any subject. A concept too bright to dull against the grindstone of normal, regular, formal, industrial-centric education.

Thanks, Mom!

Thanks, Dad!

George Hiram Gilbertson – thank you for the inspiration to audition specialties! You could do so many things well!

Civilization presses humans into a specialty, to be the best specialist that you can be. When being a generalist is humanity at its foundation best. Different kinds of "best."

Primalization, across ancestral years, adapted humans into generalist survivors. That's what I aimed for across a lifetime, with your model to guide me!

Thanks, Dad!

Thanks, for being parents with grandparent wisdom!

Foreword

As a physician interested in the meaning we construct as we go about our too short lives, I have worked in emergency rooms, intensive care units, and psychiatry wards. Ever watching and trying to understand: what we were doing, why we were doing it, and what we felt while we were at work and play.

I met Roger Gilbertson some years ago, an Engineering Duty Admiral, who was also interested in what we were doing and what we felt. We shared a common degree, Engineering, but had taken different trails since his years at Georgia Tech and mine at the Naval Academy. We were both Engineers who had gone on different roads but still shared a passion and drive to learn one more "new" or "more refined" way of looking at things.

Admiral Gilbertson is a true renaissance man but I was most drawn to Roger in his role as a philosopher-anthropologist. He was simply superb and drew my attention to 5,000,000 years of group behavior: particularly the intimacy, affection, and complicity we felt in small hunter-gatherer groups. We told stories constructing narratives so we could find breakfast and not be breakfast...narratives to sustain us and hold each other close as we spun off in space toward the unknown.

Roger has been a great teacher. His model for the group, talking around that fire burning in the night, protecting against the unknown, makes more sense than any other model I have.

I thank him for his friendship and his great humor, clarity and passion for learning. And for looking at things across the long haul.

Roger, you turned a bright light on for me during a dark night.

Captain Ronald Earl Smith, MD, PhD
United States Navy (Retired)
Washington, DC – September 2012

15

Roger Gilbertson

Preface

You and I have so many differences! – our personal micro-cultures. We live in a society that gives us choices in staggering numbers. We clutch some. Each selection gives us another dimension – as non-selection does, too.

Unknown we are. Trying to negotiate ideas through our lack of knowledge about each other. Hindered because I'm doing the "talking" and you are "listening." But at your own pace, timing and mental texture.

My speculations are many – half a century of auditioning specialties – giving a generalist's view of the cosmos.

That's what this book is about. People in uncertain connection trying to communicate ideas. A multiple set of transient, moving targets. My speculations shift and change at the edges, at the margins – rapidly. So this document is a snapshot of the moment of my writing.

I feel a need to get something "out there."

My preference is an m-book, molecular, physical, real to encourage focus, attention, reflection.

E-books are a virtual presence. Cater to other forms – other functions – transient mind-space. Spark-fast with little chance for slow, flamed-lighted knowledge.

I'm wary of the World Wide Web and the Internet. The blogs, forums, websites – encourage a too quick response to any provoking thought, some thinking needs incubation.

This m-book is more me. Yet there might be an e-version.

For me writing is an ongoing experiment in self-coaching to better tell a story, mostly to myself.

My favorite story-telling mode is: Interactive dialogue – a conversation with a person, or people.

I've given a couple thousand speeches in my lifetime.

In this book ideas are committed to writing on paper – to go through your eyes to your mind. As you see fit.

Rather than words into the air for ears. A different channel.

The goal of this work is to consider the ancient "then" culture of our ancestors as a contrast to the "now" culture of specialty-craving Civilization.

"Then" Primalization Into "Now" Civilization – "A Free-Range Human in a Caged World." Me in Civilization. You, too.

My lifetime background has given me a foundation for these speculations.

My view of the world is still seen through the eyes of a child. My interest and curiosity is childlike. Thanks again, Mom!

Humans today can not mature into a culture. Technology changes so fast – as individuals we lag behind the whirling complexity that surrounds us. Humans are outrun by tools.

What's a Finagle Watcher Book?

Humans do more than just fight or flight. We also finagle, manipulate, between fight or flight. Depending on whether our instant status is predator or prey, shifting with the moment.

Finagles take us from Primalization deeper into Civilization, challenging the human ability to survive. Eongated finagle time is what adapts us deeper into Civilization.

My goal is more books to explore that idea. Follow-on books will be shorter. This first one gave me a chance to learn more about the book crafting specialty.

Introduction

My life-sense alignment is toward Primalization – although I have done well enough – cocooned among the specifications of Civilization. This book mind-incubated for many years.

Writing helps me crystallize thought. I write as a proactive generalist – my life-time plan to sample many specialties. Moving on for new lessons when I've learned enough of the bright edges and soft center of a selected action domain.

Writing big documents is a specialty – so crafting this document required me to learn some new skills to surround content with a context. An author tends to be a specialist.

The fundamental issue for me is: will this help me grow – to be more human? Benefit for you? More food for thought?

A book is like a long, extended introduction for speaking to a group. Useful to a group? Depends on your response.

Thank You – For Your Interest – In Reading This!

Short – Punchy

My writing is purposely not scholarly. I write to understand – as simply as I can. If you want more complex supporting information the Internet is crammed full of interesting leads.

A few well chosen search words will bring a flood of information – answer some questions – stimulate more questions. The World Wide Web is the place to mine for the knowledge nuggets that fit your personal speculations the best.

My goal is to be broad, not deep.

I know many of the formal writing rules and often bend them for a different clarity.

Declarative Sentences

I mostly write short declarative sentences. The kind Winston Churchill loved. Full of direct speculation.

I punctuate the way I feel. I use Capitalization whenever it seems good to Highlight something.

Inspiration

Inspiration often comes to me early in the morning. That's when I have best access to the creativity of my calm, slow, brain waves, in a way that associates ideas.

Inspiration also comes when I talk to people. Feedback from other minds improves my thoughts. So does reading – but without the quick real-time feedback of conversation.

A goal is to keep up with threads of culture and nature: anthropology – cosmology – brain research – leadership – science – art – music. A daunting, always incomplete, enjoyable task set.

Generalist Writer

My personal choice has been to develop as a generalist. My story shows progress toward that goal. Disclosing enough so you can understand me better, in this short time, with this fragile connection. My basic nature is cooperation not competition.

A proactive generalist through multiple specializations.

Most details and sharp near focus are left to the experts. And I appreciate their devotion to uncovering facts to share.

They are out there creating "their truth"- personal point-of-view knowledge – to sample – and latch into the "fish hooks" of the associative memories of others.

Trying for a broad focus on the mental pictures that make up a mosaic, "A Big Picture," for approximation into "My Big Picture." Connecting selected specialty dots with broad strokes: a cascading interleaved matrix in the mind.

Is it a paradox to be a generalist writer?

Probably. So I'm a generalist struggling to do this writing specialty beyond my usual audition.

I write my talk – a dialog – with you. If you know how I sound I hope you can "hear" my voice flipping through these words. I'm sorry you can't talk back!

Numbers

Many of the comparison numbers I use are subject to interpretation. We learn as we classify, to measure – as we progress through time. So change keeps coming: numbers – time – place – details – ideas – fundamentals.

Numbers are useful to give a sense of scale – and spice up writing. Numbers insert one sort of thought in the mind – letters stimulate another.

I tend to use direct numbers so they stand out from words. No need for the mental translation from "numbers as words" – to slow up thinking.

To me "2" looks more immediately – appropriately – numeric than "two."

The same goes for "seven billion" – I usually write: "7,000,000,000."

The numbers call out to you: "Look at me! I'm the measure of something! Don't let the words hide me!"

Yet the number sometimes seems more than it is. A number appears precise. Often there is really a range that a specific number only represents.

An example: When I say there were 40 people in a gathering hunting band – I speculate that some bands were as small as 20 – or as large as 80. Often numbers are hints at size – and precision is an illusion.

Compare

Word-Intensive

```
The gathering hunting tribal clan of six
hundred people - ten thousand years ago -
contrasts with a world population today of
seven billion.  Our bodies then and now were
composed of about seventy trillion cells.
With each cell containing a strand of DNA
maybe six feet long - with a blueprint message
of about four billion letters.
```

Number-Spiced

```
The tribal clan of 600 people - 10,000 years
ago - contrasts today with 7,000,000,000.  Our
bodies then and now were composed of about
70,000,000,000,000 cells.  With each cell
containing a strand of DNA maybe 6 feet long -
with a blueprint message of about
4,000,000,000 letters.
```

Why Gathering Hunting?

Traditionally the terminology is hunting before gathering in most literature. For me, "gathering" feels right to be first. Humans were gathering long before we hunted. Our ancestors gathered, foraged, scavenged, and hunted for a long time.

Part 1 – Free-Range Human

What life events are guiding me – across 75+ years – to do this brand of speculation?

Chapter 1 – Why Me?

What has life been like, moving through the choice-rich culture of America – while imbedded in the larger Caged World of Civilization?

Why is Civilization trying to cage us? While living immersed mostly in the United States I have been increasingly aware of the pot-holed detours from Primalization.

What early beginnings shifted me toward broad ideas about Primalization? Why think about the Primal Metaphor?

Why am I the right person for thinking – writing – talking about this issue? Am I credible?

My 200% Mother

"Thank you, Mom!" Myrtle Julianna Gunderson Gilbertson. "All that I do rests on the unique start in life that you gave me."

My greatest stroke of chance was being born to a mother who used instinct to raise me. Not the theories being written, by men, about child rearing in the 1930s.

My mother did not smoke. Did not drink alcohol. Did not use caffeine. Neither did Dad.

My mother did not add salt or pepper or spice to anything she cooked or fed us in the family. Just plain food.

She made desserts – with sugar – only at special events, usually pies at Christmas, Easter, and Thanksgiving. She made cakes for Birthdays. Not much extra sugar.

When she was pregnant with me I had healthy blood from Mom's shared supply for us both. Her diet protected me.

Then in my early life these are some of her gifts to me:

- mother's milk – breast-feeding – calming oasis – available until I was 4 years old

- home-made baby food – salt-free, sugar-free – starting at 6 months

- sleeping in the family bed until my sister came along

- free-range, exploration-rich, toddler-living with no confining "play" pen or stroller

- only family members as baby-sitters

- encouraged to walk and talk at about 1 year

- taught to read with phonics before I remember

- at age 10 – Sunburst Diagramming – linear and random – left-brain and right-brain graphic thinking

- a lust for learning

- a love of molecular books substance that fits me

- never spanked, never punished, taught with rewards

- Mom gave me excellent life coaching until she passed away in her 94th year

- a negative? The impossible expectation of having a lifetime in a real gathering hunting band.

- Thus – too much clutter where humans should be

One-Room School House Teacher

Myrtle Gilbertson started teaching in a one-room school house in 1918 in rural Wisconsin.

Her school had grades 1 to 8, with about a dozen children – all in one classroom, with one teacher. A vertical knowledge refining group. Only 1 or 2 kids of the same age. The older helped teach the younger – and watched out for them.

She ended her career 52 years later at age 70 in an inner city school in Baltimore, Maryland. In an "Industrial Revolution, Raise-Your-Hand to Ask-For-Permission" regular school.

She took time out to be with each of her own kids. Mom was a master teacher – and I was her only student from 1936 to 1941, from zero to 5. By the time my sister came along I was reading on my own – gathering and hunting knowledge. Just playing, to become an adult – no extra pressure.

Because my sister was born in 1941 – Mom continued at home from 1936 to 1946 to be with Beverly until she was 5.

Mom's Gunderson Ancestors

The Gundersons came to the United States in 1868. They left Lillehammer, Norway – sailed to Liverpool, England – then embarked on a sailing ship for the month long trip.

The Homestead Act was only 6 years old. My ancestors searched for land that felt like Norway. They homesteaded a farm near Price in northern Wisconsin. My mother grew up on that farm – close to agriculture not urbanization. She was self-sufficient and self-assured. She had 7 brothers and sisters – a mini-gathering hunting band in itself. The Gundersons had a long tradition of farming in Norway.

25

My 99% Father

I am the son of George Gilbertson. He served in The Great War, World War I. He was called up to serve in the Mexican Border Campaign in 1916 and then in 1917 for the World War.

George was a Revenuer during Prohibition from 1923 to 1933. He continued after Prohibition ended, a Revenue Agent with the U.S. Treasury Department until retirement in 1953.

I call him the 99% father because he was kind and loving most of the time – but flew into a rage about 4 times a year. One was usually around Christmas.

That meant I learned to walk on eggs around him. I did not want to set him off. Usually I loved him – occasionally I hated him. Perhaps he had trench warfare "shell shock," the term used in World War One for Post Traumatic Stress (PTS).

The advantage was that I learned to deal with difficult people, wherever I came across them.

Auditioning Specialties

When my Dad left home at age 16 in 1904 he worked in many jobs in many places around the Old West. He worked as a cowboy – in the wheat fields – building a railroad – felling timber – constructing buildings. Whatever needed to be done.

He worked in Wisconsin, Minnesota, the Dakotas, Montana, Idaho, Washington, Oregon, California, Arizona, and New Mexico. He "rode the rails," hopping a train to a new place.

He was a young adventurer. He joined the National Guard in Minneapolis in 1915 – after 11 years of auditioning specialties. He served in the desert of the Mexican Border Campaign before he fought in the trenches of World War I France as a Machine Gun Sergeant.

When he got home from the Great War – he married my mother. They started a family. My brother, Warren, was born in 1921.

They auditioned farming near Eau Claire, Wisconsin, and both went to college.

After trying enough specializations – Dad joined the Internal Revenue Service at age 35. He loved the variety of seeking and finding moonshiners and bootleggers. He enjoyed investigating – doing undercover work – testifying in court – being mostly away from "the office." In the outside. Never a dull moment, he roamed a territory seeking changed patterns.

Dad's Gilbertson Ancestors

Gilbert Gilbertson was my great-grandfather, born in 1821. Gilbert was an early deep sea diver. The full diving suit was invented in 1838, when Gilbert was 17. He was living in the right place, Horton, Norway, very close to the North Sea with plenty of underwater adventure.

My father told the story of Gilbert being the only survivor of 2 shipwrecks. My genes hang by a slim thread of chance.

My Gilbertson ancestors also came to America shortly after the Civil War, also settling on homestead land. Much like the Gundersons. Dad had 8 brothers and sisters.

Eventually the Gilbertsons and the Gundersons were on farms about a mile apart – near Price, Wisconsin. That's how my parents met.

Blended Family

"Little House On The Prairie" meets "The Untouchables" - those were two early television series.

Myrtle Gunderson taught in that one-room schoolhouse adjacent to her family homestead – thus, "Little House on the Prairie" and George Gilbertson was a Revenue Agent during Prohibition – an "Untouchable."

They both clung to documents – some that I have go back to when Myrtle and George were newly-weds. In 1941, George built a storeroom in the basement of our house in Eau Claire, Wisconsin, and saved books and paper work. We moved away later that year but kept the house for another 60 years.

My brother and I went through some of the boxes and found our father's case file for events and adventures from his years enforcing Prohibition. We also came across planning books from my mother's one-room school house days. Both parents gave me inspiration to be an information-collector and knowledge-crafter. Yup, with too much clutter.

They were married for 50 years. Dad died in 1971 – his 84th year and Mom died in 1993 – her 94th year. They taught me to seek the ragged edges of new learning.

Decisions Made Long Before Me

Out of Africa

This decision was made by our human ancestors at least 40,000 years ago – when early man left Africa for a variety of settings. There are lots of opinions about the timing.

Early humans did a series of divestitures – as gathering hunting tribal clans became too successful and grew. The neighborhood would become over-crowded with us. Not enough land for more people in the same place.

The resulting population pressure would have moved some to all the other continents to set up new home territory.

28

Into Norway

Sometime – as the last Ice Age began to melt – my more immediate ancestors headed into the North – into what became Norway, most likely within the last few thousand years.

Vikings

My Dad's ancestors from Horton would have been Vikings. Maybe that's where my dad inherited his need to rage: some Vikings were berserkers who rage-fought in the now moment.

Horton, Norway, is in the area where the Vikings sailed forth into the world's seas. Perhaps part of why I joined the Navy – and eventually retired as a Rear Admiral.

Agriculture

My mother's early family were farmers in the agricultural center of Norway at Lillehammer.

The church records there go back to the beginning of Christianity in Norway – documenting my recent ancestors.

Decision-Flow With Fundamental Impact on Me

Homesteading in Wisconsin

Both sides of the family left Norway, crossed the Atlantic as passengers on sailing ships, decided on going to Wisconsin and homesteaded. Part of my heritage was set. Do what you can with what you have – but also explore.

Self-Sufficient Parenting

My parents developed the sense, and the habits, of being self-sufficient pioneers over 100 years ago. My Dad was born in

1888 and my Mom in 1899. They also survived the Great Depression with its thrift-enhancing "lessons learned."

Mom and Dad Together as My Parents

My Mom was a young teacher and my Dad a veteran home from the World War. They got married and started a family.

Home Un-Schooled Until Near Age 7

My mother took time out for her children. From 1921 for a few years for my brother and from 1936 for my sister and me. My mother let me play at becoming an adult at home until the first grade. I was prepared with the essence of self-learning.

Folks Sent Me Into Baltimore for My Education

My Mom studied local school systems and determined that the Baltimore City schools were better for me than the County of Baltimore – where we lived then. So that's where I went. It was another jurisdiction so my folks budgeted tuition for my decade in that system. That decision gave me access to Baltimore Poly – a superb engineering high school.

Friends in the Neighborhood and Elementary School

I had 4 groups of friends to socialize with: the home neighborhood and 3 groups in elementary school because I skipped a full grade in 2 halves. Auditioning social groups – learning to convert new strangers into new friends.

Left Junior High School A Year Early

Gwynnes Falls Junior High School recommended that I leave a year early to attend the magnet engineering high school in Baltimore. My parents agreed and I started attending the Baltimore Polytechnic Institute when I was 13.

Baltimore Poly 'A' Course

I was placed in the Accelerated program – the "A" Course at Poly. So from 1950 to 1954 I got an excellent preparatory school education. We studied math, science, and engineering, plus literature, history, and liberal arts. "Accelerated" meant that when I graduated from Poly I also had completed the freshman year of engineering college.

The decision to go to Poly, an hour commute away by 2 city buses and a trackless trolley, was critical for later activities. I'm grateful for the wisdom of my parents.

There was also luck involved.

The decisions after Poly were made with my majority input.

The result contributed to a lifetime of many disciplines – cross pollination – multi macro tasking.

Books

Along the way I've appreciated books as idea generators, enough to have obvious "book clutter." I've "mined" many more than I've read cover to cover, looking for nuggets that fit my thought patterns.

My speculations are a personal recipe of morsels plucked from many places, people, experience, articles – with books giving versions of earlier frozen thoughts. My book exposure shows me the fundamental ideas that humans have are universal.

The way those concepts are organized, strung together, and expressed makes the difference. Shifts in metaphor from one idea to another are often re-labeled in a changing culture as new. Thus regrinding the flour of ideas into an ever finer dust, old concepts with brighter life in a new context.

31

Now I also do a lot of Web surfing. There are lots of ideas being reground and repackaged and reignited on the Internet.

Yet "the molecular book" remains my favorite – fully portable – no extra energy needed – you can write in your copy – it cues memory by its physical presence – and that mbook can go on to an intellectual afterlife. Perhaps many reincarnations in other minds. Idea hunting in used book stores is a favorite pastime.

Books Are Like a Hunt - Articles Like a Gather

Books take hours to read, require concentration, are complex, are resource hungry. Articles take minutes to read, are simpler, are gathered in journals and magazines. Books take longer to write and have greater economic and celebrity pay-off.

Why craft a book length document?

Authors write what they think is worth reading, a lonely task. Alone with the writing – with enough self-possession to think someone will read what they wrote. I'm writing this, partly, at the request of folks who have heard me talk.

All writing is a form of autobiography. We write what we know and care about, a form of self-disclosure.

Authors – and leaders, celebrities, politicians, entertainers – find expanding emotional seams in a culture and play to that opportunity. Published authors have self-knowledge and other-knowledge to write with a plausible reader target.

I don't presume a recipe for "writing success" since what I craft is mostly to understand myself. Writing sharpens my thoughts.

Auto-biographical lists about me come later – in telegraphic style. Those lists thread the mosaic of influences on my life's journey.

Perhaps that will help you decide I have speculations useful to you – ping pong aphorisms.

Generalist

I think of myself as a successful generalist. I have consciously avoided the cultural goals of gathering wealth and hunting celebrity status. Dollar fortune and wide fame seem to tempt a personality to corrosion – with exaggerated self-worth, in a culture afloat in manipulating flattery.

My Life Vision Decision – Fall of 1955

By the Fall of 1955 I was studying in my 4th quarter at Georgia Tech and had worked for 3 quarters as a cooperative student at Bendix Radio. During that pivotal Fall I took the first digital computer course ever offered at Georgia Tech – taught in the Math Department. I was also taking another course taught by a Japanese teacher who was newly arrived in the United States.

I decided that I wanted to know from plus infinity to minus infinity in an infinity of dimensions, a broad vision. Being an engineering specialist felt too narrow, confining. I needed to:

- Audition specialties in education, geography, and occupations
- Aim at understanding regional patterns of thought in the United States
- Explore the nature of other countries
- Participate in the digital revolution
- Become a multi-specialist – thus a generalist

That's when I took over life shifting decisions on my own. Up until then my folks shaped most decisions. Advice was still requested, and often taken, but I owned my destiny.

Continuous Lifelong Reinvention

The result has been a lifetime of reinvention to take on new issues, new opportunities, new challenges.

Continuous Lifelong Learning

Experience and formal education interconnect across a lifetime. The formal education always balanced against developing practical factors learned in the reality of experience.

Rare – But Not That Rare

The generalist in Civilization seemed more common in the era of my folks. Yet I have come across other generalists every now and then during my lifetime. Sometimes they have lots of degrees that have given them access into various domains of life. Sometimes they have lots of skills with no degrees and can do many things.

Formal education sends what Civilization wants you to know. Experience gives what you need to know.

Generalists often have energetic, open spirits of adventure for experience and education.

The Wild Generalists

Fundamental natural generalists, real gatherers and hunters, continue to exist. On the Island of Borneo, in the Amazon Rain Forest, in remote parts of Africa, and possibly elsewhere. With remnant, lifeboat knowledge about near-wild nature. In a needy future they might save our species from the unexpected perils of over-technology.

Wild generalists become rarer as their local refuge lands become wealth targets for remote, unconcerned others.

So what?

Civilization places every human inhabitant in a stressed condition through too rapid cultural change.

Every child raised in Civilization has been neglected – by the standard of Primalization. The process of development in a growing human body can be confused by the changes demanded by Civilization: specialization – competition – technology – population – strangers.

Nature and nurture are both critical – and in constant negotiation with each other – producing a unique "you."

The body and the mind will try to keep-up with culture and thus be in prolonged stress – usually at a continuous low level – occasionally at a high level.

The characteristics of a gathering hunting band life style can give a sense of what can be done to decrease the stress. Finding a balance depends on choice. Choices are many.

Negotiating with all your modern "surrogate gathering hunting bands" is important. What is feasible for you?

You are a member of many modern bands not just the birth band or the embraced band you would have had in Primalization. The result is very few people sense or can access the "real" you. Or even guess at the real you.

You may not know yourself. Defined by a mix of forces that have transformed you across a lifetime.

Strangers all around – perhaps even "your self" to you.

You Are a Stranger

You are a stranger – surrounded by strangers – most with a primary specialty unlike yours. Much of your social time is spent negotiating with chance strangers.

Drawing personal lines to define the boundaries of your "Primalization within Civilization" is a lifetime enterprise.

Balance in life – family – work – education – the spirit – physical – mental – is not easy. Picking what makes sense, or even if choices make sense, are an individual's finest options.

Finding yourself. Defining yourself.

In America we have vast panoramas of choice.

About all a human can do is speculate – and decide which other speculators seem trustworthy. Each of us lives in our own individualized, unique micro-culture.

Based on a progressive series of incrementally informed personal speculations.

If my explorations in speculation help – I'm glad!

Some of what I express disturbs people with a different worldview.

Some of what I write disturbs me.

Speculation is probability-based – never certain.

Good luck!

In all you do!

Chapter 2 – Life Textures

Here are lists that provide the threads woven into a life texture for me. How I've aimed at being a generalist while surrounded by specialists.

My agenda was to audition selected specialties. Then gain enough knowledge to add skills to my tool kit – then move on to the next fenced, grazing knowledge meadow. To become a multi-specialist, a generalist. Lists give a fast-paced quick-look.

A Life Cascade of Decisions

- Go to Georgia Tech
- Join a Fraternity
- Become a Generalist
- Stay in Engineering for a Degree
- Go To Purdue
- Select the University of Colorado
- Join the Navy
- Audition GWU Law School
- Leave Navy Active Duty
- Continue in the Naval Reserve
- Participate in the Cold War in the Navy
- Get Married & Start a Family
- Form A Futures Consulting Firm
- Run for Congress
- Become a Management Consultant
- Enter Federal Civil Service
- Go to the Harvard Business School
- Audition California
- Leave a Banking Executive Position

37

- Return to Washington
- Reject "Non-Calling" Opportunities
- Maintain Parallel Careers
- Raise a Family
- Continue Formal Education
- Maintain International Geographic Interests
- Participate in the Hot Peace & the Cold War
- Start Volunteer Credit Union Commitment
- Serve in the White House
- Stay in International Trade Administration
- Earn a Doctorate from USC – Southern Cal
- Focus on Generalist Fundamentals
- Study Philosophy
- Study Psychology
- Study Anthropology
- Study Leadership
- Study Followership
- Understand Primalization
- Keep Trying Things in Civilization
- Turn Down Executive Recruiters
- Accept Waiver of Navy Mandatory Retirement
- Realign from Civilian Federal Service
- Start Writing & Speaking as an Elder

Experience Thread

Here are some of my titles through the years that hint at a lifetime of generalist experience:

- Senior Crossing Guard at P.S. 220
- Homeroom Vice President
- Draftsman
- Surveyor
- Engineer

38

- Researcher
- Social Chairman
- Door-to-Door Salesman
- Residence Hall Faculty Sponsor
- Assistant Section Leader
- Naval Officer
- Bull Ensign
- Program Manager
- Technical Representative
- Entrepreneur
- Chief Executive Officer
- Chairman of the Board
- Futures Consultant
- Civic Association President
- Congressional Candidate
- Management Consultant
- Fraternity District Governor
- Planning, Programming, Budgeting Consultant
- Administrative Officer
- Director of Program Planning
- Director, Program Information Management
- Management-Labor Director
- Can Group Leader
- Director of Planning
- Executive Officer
- Management Information Consultant at the White House
- Commanding Officer
- Alumni Association President
- Local Secretary
- Class Vice President
- Adjunct Professor
- Retirement Fund Trustee
- Venture Capitalist
- Program Manager for Basic Research
- Chairman of the Board Emeritus

- Rear Admiral – Lower Half
- Leader – Navy "High Tech Brain Trust"
- Rear Admiral – 2 Stars
- Seminar Leader
- Public Speaker
- Writer
- Thinker
- Incrementally Informed Personal Speculator
- Thriving Generalist
- Interpreter of Ancient Wisdom

Educational Influences

Formal education gives clues about what a culture thinks is important, and the directions of its indoctrination. Some of my school programs were for years and degrees – others for shorter auditions – weeks or months. Trying on specialties.

- 1936 Born into the United States
- 1943 Mom's Gift: UnSchooled at Home for about 7 years
- 1948 Morrell Park, PS 220
- 1950 Gwynnes Falls Junior High
- 1954 Baltimore Poly High School
- 1958 Georgia Tech
- 1959 Purdue University
- 1961 University of Colorado
- 1961 Navy Officers Candidate School
- 1964 George Washington University Law School
- 1967 American University
- 1972 Harvard Business School
- 1975 UCLA
- 1986 & 1988 University of Southern California
- 1990 Industrial College of the Armed Forces
- 1993 Army War College

40

- 1993 National Defense University Capstone
- 1995 Taught at Shenandoah University
- 1994 Defense Systems Management College
- 1997 Harvard Kennedy School of Government

Academic Recognition

- Eta Kappa Nu – Electrical Engineering – Georgia Tech
- Alpha Pi Mu – Industrial Engineering – Georgia Tech
- Briaerian Society – Co-op Students – Georgia Tech
- Dean's List – Georgia Tech
- Pi Sigma Alpha – Political Science – U. of Colorado
- "Newport Presentation Sword" as First of 300 – Navy Officers Candidate School
- Pi Alpha Alpha – Public Administration – University of Southern California

Attachments to these States & DC

- Wisconsin – North Carolina – Maryland
- Georgia – Indiana – Colorado
- Rhode Island – Minnesota – Virginia – DC
- Massachusetts
- California
- Washington – Oregon – Hawaii

Language Exposure

- English – My native language
- Norwegian – Heard often as a child – no fluency
- French – Took in high school – still a rank beginner
- Esperanto – Interesting ideas – no fluency

- Computer Languages – Programmed in 64 of them

Music

- Piano – A few lessons
- Accordion – Just enough lessons to start
- Voice – Untaught but love to sing big band era songs
- Pre-Dawn Jazz Listener for energizing
- Classical Music Listener for calming

Sports

Played sand-lot:

- Baseball
- Soccer
- Football
- Volleyball

Played frozen pond:

- Ice Hockey

Got Good at:

- Free-Style Figure Skating (Ice and Roller)
- Jitter Bug Dancing

Art

- Figurative Abstracts
- Photographic Abstracts

Incrementally Informed Personal Speculation

Incrementally informed speculation – the core of humankind's advances in knowledge. We inch forward until we have a "punctuated increment".

We are all equals, all dealing with speculations. Some humans feel their own personal speculations are better than the speculations of others – could be. My sense is we are all in this together as equals. Living our adventure. Crafting our speculations – and specializations – as we live through a life.

There was profound agreement in a gathering hunting band during Primalization, little personal choice. Each of us today, in living generations, is surrounded by choice. We each have our own personal micro-culture, in Civilization. We slowly, sometimes gently, step into deeper isolation as we live a life journey without many traveling companions. Our lessons-learned tend to be our own – personal – alone.

Some of my auditioning of pieces of living included digesting books. Over about 28,000 days of life I've owned about 12,500 books. In the early days I read some from front to back, in a linear way, as Civilization would suggest. I have "mined for nuggets of knowledge" in maybe another 40,000.

The book mining process is non-linear – looking for the sparks of direct generalist interest to me. So I check the index, the table of contents, scan for headings, look for images, graphs, tables, charts, numbers. So I'll know what to target. Then read – or scan – what seems to fit me.

I look at the index first because the alphabetic texture is not as controlled by the author. The table of contents is the author's designed playground – the index is my sandbox.

That is "Primalization reading." Non-linear – generalist idea feeding – to a rhythm – harmonizing the "song of a book" with my "song of a life."

My mission in speculation since my personal 1955 "Eureka" has been to try knowing "exponential infinity." This clearly can not be done, yet is a process – a vision – a mission – with purpose – into flow.

Forging ahead among crafted words – book mining. Loose objective oriented. Serendipity seeking. I feel like the poster elder for multi-disciplined learning – thinking – searching.

Plus lots of discussion with many other people – a great unstructured concept source. Making intellectual stew.

Agreed Group Speculation

Groups of humans move in mental directions inspired by individuals who chance into leadership. If a person has a strong, well-tuned follower network then personal speculations can influence a group for long stretches of time. Differing cultures, values, ideas, countries, and religions can persist.

The speculation can be about tools, how to live, what to believe, who to trust, why to act – basic issues that engage an individual's brain space and influence life tempo.

Credibility

Thank you for giving me some of your time, mind-attention, and brain-space.

Speculations follow after this quick look at my life flow. My right-brained thoughts on Primalization are expressed as contrasts with the linear left-brain Civilization we live within.

You'll probably disagree with some of what I have to say.

My outlook tends toward optimistic skepticism. Yet we all have a micro-culture that defines "the you," in your mind. Your ideas are as good for you as mine are for me.

Specialists tend to feel an ownership of their specialty. My "ownership" is more about inquiry and curiosity and expression – rather than intellectual property. Yet I do copyright.

Civilization creates stresses about most life options. Creating property value from the exchange of ideas forms stress in the "full cooperation" part of me.

Organization Savvy

There are elements here that might help individuals among modern grouped humans. Family. Friends. Colleagues.

To better understand how you fit into Civilization.

To help modern human bands find community and individual fulfillment.

To be a personal "success" by your own definition.

To get survival resources.

To make a "profit" – as you gauge it.

Preview of Coming Attractions

Next let's take a look at the contrasts – simple Primalization compared to complex Civilization with all of its negotiations, intentions, and compromises made across many generations.

Primalization highlights the role of humanity without many external tools but lots of internal skills.

Civilization looks at humans encased in many rapidly evolving complex tools. Each with its own bling – "a want" often manipulated into "a need."

The many products of fast moving technology morphed into requirements because "it's there."

Science is never still – never silent. Each new abstract finding has an immediate demand to be converted into a profitable real object – a tool.

High tech at work.

Perhaps our tools own us.

A mesh of tools with humans enveloped in the net.

Habits keep our tools perhaps too near – too ready.

Many tools seem to have an immediate short-range benefit and a delayed long-range cost.

Now gain.

For later pain.

The cost often skips into following generations of humans. Grandchildren pay for the decisions of their grandparents.

Much that we now do seems to need balance in the muddled middle between nature and nurture – Primalization and Civilization.

You are caught between the accumulated lessons learned by your ancient ancestors and active dealings with the people you are imbedded among – today.

For Me It Has Been A Full Life
Been There, Tried That
Jack Of Many Trades, Master Of Some

Part 2 – Caged World

Civilization today cages all of us, blossoming out after the invention of agriculture – about 10,000 years ago.

Chapter 3 – Gathering Hunting Bands & Tribal Clans

How did our long-ago ancestors live in gathering hunting bands nestled within tribal clans? "Gathering" logically comes first – we've done it much longer. Hunting was later.

Distant in time and place. Long ago – and far away. Back beyond 500 generations for most humans alive today.

Remote in detail. Foggy at best. Yet imaginable. Food for our speculation.

A Savanna Story

A gathering hunting band is walking across the savanna. When seen from above, is a task force on an ocean of grass – near a sprinkle of trees along stream lines.

In the middle are 20 children and 10 women. Around the edge are 10 men – the security force that protects the vital center. The children represent the only profit – survival for our species into the future.

Everyone is naked – and they all look very much alike. They share the same food and about the same genes. The men are a few inches taller than the women. They all have an athletic body style – well muscled – no fat. Eating what's right – what's naturally available. Walking a lot.

They are alert to every pattern in their surroundings.

Suddenly a man on the left loud-grunts a warning. He starts racing toward the lion that is charging the band. The women marshal the children, ready for anything.

The other men head for the lion, running toward the danger.

They know how this individual lion will respond. He slows when the men begin converging in front of him. The men don't act like prey. They don't flee! They look him in the eye from a higher, superior, height.

They seem ready to fight.

The lion expects to running down frightened animals – looking for a way to safety. Not these humans looking toward him.

Perhaps even moving toward him.

Plus there's more than one, a cooperating group.

They don't even seem scared.

The lion does not have a single target for focus.

It is much easier to pick off fleeing prey.

The old – young – slow – sick – weak – alone – or unlucky – fall to the lion's bite.

The easy-prey herd always outruns the one that will die.

The lion stops – turns – and walks away.

Confronted by too many human eyes – looking down at him.

Too many people with height-of-eye advantage.

Too many targets not running away.

Humans know the secret of a joint stand. Cooperation!

The lion will find easier food in another place.

He has the speed, the strength, and the teeth for it – but not the brain to take on something as uncertain as grouped humans.

The tactic worked – this time, and most times.

Not just fight or flight, add our human option: finagle.

Or we would not be here.

We ranged the East Side of Africa for millions of years.

Bluffing still works – for lots of humans – now worldwide.

Presently we manipulate, we bluff, we fight, we flee, and we finagle, but now usually among each other.

The hunter-killers we lived among on the savannas are gone.

Caged in zoos.

Hunted to extinction or isolation.

Or domesticated.

Today we are our own prey and predator.

Sometimes one, sometimes the other, depending on blended context. Fast moving mental stances.

The Extended Story
Humans have come a long way.

Since 5,000,000 years
- Walked upright on 2 long legs
- Developed a 4 times larger brain – in the last 2,500,000 years
- Started making tools – about 1,800,000 years ago
- Shifted from exclusively gathering and foraging
- Added scavenging then hunting, killing for ourselves

- Added fishing, hunting prey in the water
- Began to control fire, perhaps 700,000 years ago
- Moved throughout Africa – maybe beyond

Since 40,000 years

- Developed a spoken language: speaking with nuance
- Crafted finer tools: faster
- Became more expressive with art
- Spread out of Africa into broader, different territory
- Developed place-sensitive cultures.

Since 10,000 years

- Started to settle into agriculture
- Stationary planting or pre-gathering
- Nomadic herding or pre-hunting
- Filled the World, while killing off the fat, big, easy prey.

Since 5,000 years

- Started living in cities
- Became surrounded by Specialized Strangers
- Started writing to capture and extend nuanced language

Primalization Into Civilization

The long-range detour we humans have taken is a journey from Primalization into Civilization, with lots of hairpin turns.

Contrasting

I'm use a style of headings and text that keep 2 kinds of speculation separate. The Primalization heading is at the left margin – the Civilization heading is *Italic* and indented. The text for Primalization is book-normal. The text for Civilization looks like a typewriter – a modern, yet obsolete invention – with ragged right margins – and a shady background.

Primalization first

After some statements about how our ancient heritage might have looked – the next heading will show how Civilization deals with the parallel situation – or issue – or idea.

Civilization second

```
From a Free-Range Culture to a Caged Culture.

The instinctive mothering I got in my very
early years gave me a sense of human belonging
- human equality.  Neither humble nor
arrogant, in the middle: equality.  Classless.

The habits of Civilization misuse the organs
of the body - overused or little used -
developed or undeveloped.

It would be the slimmest chance for any single
human to have all systems mature as they would
have in Primalization.

Among the most misshaped must be the mind -
our brain under chemical siege - its
```

remembered contents crafted from off-centered cultures over many generations.

My early start with a natural mother gave me some shelter from habits indoctrinated from the surrounding culture. Yet Civilized culture is too powerful to avoid for long.

Our culture has placed me in a cage like all of us, only it took a while longer to do it. I feel only partially caged. Thus have some freedom to mind-roam.

I'm trying to be a free-range thinker and doer where I can.

You'll see what I mean as you read along.

Chapter 4 – Fundamental Contrasts

Cooperation

Cooperation – this is the most important characteristic that humans maintained during Primalization. For most of the last 5,000,000 years, we have shared everything.

We had togetherness that is hard to imagine in Civilization. The same gathering hunting tribal clan of 600 people was our lifetime home. To us that 600 was all of humanity.

Our genes were all very close. Our diet was about the same. We learned the same lessons from our culture. Our territory was a small patch of savanna, wandering among water, food and safety sources. We were near the Equator on the East side of the Great Rift in Africa.

We were seldom more than 50 feet from our birth gathering hunting band of 40 people. Those are important numbers – 40 in a gathering band – 600 in a tribal clan.

Competition

Civilization is driving us ever nearer to individual competition among other humans.

Our genes now come from all over the world. Our diets are ad-driven, and full of chemicals. The lessons we learn are mostly from our own individual experience. Our territory is large. We live in intense cold, and in high heat – Arctic to Tropic.

Competition among solo people insulates – individualizes – isolates. Hard to share anything without a profit motive. Can we move

back to cooperation? How much? We do need to
compete!

The competition should probably be against
strangers - not against family and friends and
colleagues.   The really close folks should be
instinctive allies. How do you get ahead if
you are too cooperative with your competing
work associates? The cooperation -
competition line shifts from moment to moment.

The struggle between cooperation and
competition is redrawn in every episode
between Civilized people. Much modern time is
spent negotiating that line. How do you guide
cooperation? Or navigate competition? Or
build mutual trust?

We all need to find a way to get resources to
live, through Civilization.

Generalists

Every member of a gathering band was a thriving generalist.

Everyone gathered.

Women and men and children all ate food that has roots..
About 80% of nutrition came from the gathering function –
plants. That's why I put it first.

Everyone hunted – women might kill small animals unlucky
enough to get in range.

Most hunting would be by men. Usually in a team of 5 or less
– so stealth would be effective.

Any difference in skill was based upon age. The older you
were the more experienced you were – indifferent to stable
technology. The set of skills remained about the same –
adapting over many generations in our wonderful mind.

Every adult had a "job description" with the same title: "Generalist." Some of the details were a little different depending on gender. Every child had critical age-dependent work to do: "Playing to Become an Adult."

Specialists

Today the task is to become a specialist – to pick a specialty – to learn it – and to get resources from Civilization for doing it.

Your contract with Civilization says if you do a particular thing very well – then you might be well paid for doing it. You do something – the culture gives you payment – maybe a lot. If you are lucky. Technology shakes the dice creating your open seam.

If you are unlucky your specialty might vanish. We live in a hyper-dynamic environment where accelerating change engulfs us. We ride the Tiger of Technology. The Tiger is hungry and unpredictable. If you guess right you stay in your personal-success saddle.

The environment is too chaotic and too deep to allow true generalists to swim in it. There are so many skills in the "coming and going" of specialties. But it is possible to be a multi-specialist – to have gates in your specialty fences. If your current "bread and butter" specialty begins to sink – then open the gate into another "field" where you have created some cross-skill with anticipation – and intent. Lucky in preparing for luck – then recognizing it.

Contrasts and tradeoffs for decisions are crafted within a broader thought-range.

```
Specialties have their own jargon - language -
mini-culture - barriers to entry.  With
different frameworks for thinking.
```

No Strangers

There were no strangers during the Primalization era.

Everyone in a gathering hunting tribal clan – the 600 – knew everyone else. That was an outer circle of "near intimates."

The inner circle was the gathering hunting band of perhaps 40 people: 10 women – 10 men – and 20 children. You knew everything about them. The 15 gathering hunting bands together made up the larger tribal clan of 600.

Usually the savanna could not provide enough food in one place to support the whole tribe at once. Each band of 40 would gather and hunt independently – most of the time. Twice a year the tribal clan of 600 could get together. Easier on the savanna than in a jungle.

When the rainy season ended it was harvest time for plants. The gathering function in one place-of-plenty could sustain all the 600 – a women's conference. When the dry season ended the migrating animals would be back with easy-to- hunt young prey. Then it was the hunter's turn to provide most food – a men's conference. Each "conference" might last from a week to a month depending on food bounty.

You had direct knowledge of your band of 40, plus "story knowledge" of your tribal clan of 600. "No strangers" because the next clan of 600 might be too far away to know. Or might not exist at all.

Surrounded by a Stranger Swarm

```
In Civilization we are surrounded by a rapidly
swirling cast of characters.  Walk down a busy
```

street of any city – you often see not a soul you know.

Yet everyone passed will be acknowledged. You seldom bump into anyone – your action is simple avoidance.

We judge strangers by how they disturb the patterns we expect. Usually visual – sometimes audio. Maybe scent. Do you want to be unknown? No!

You want 40 people near in a very tight inner circle – 600 in the looser outer circle.

As strangers to others we crave social attention – to be full-time members of a group – to not be unknown – a powerful double negative.

The hunger for celebrity – for fame – even notoriety, is an attempt to get back to when we all knew everyone. When you had the trust of all around you.

Now we know that today's "everyone" is 7,000,000,000 not yesterday's 600.

The one-to-many ratio between a celebrity and fans is corrosive. The many can't know the "real" one.

One-to-one: is the truer human ratio. Eye-to-eye. Or one-to-a few. Eye-to-known eyes.

Anywhere, you always recognize an old friend.

The known face is human pattern-recognized in any swarm crowd.

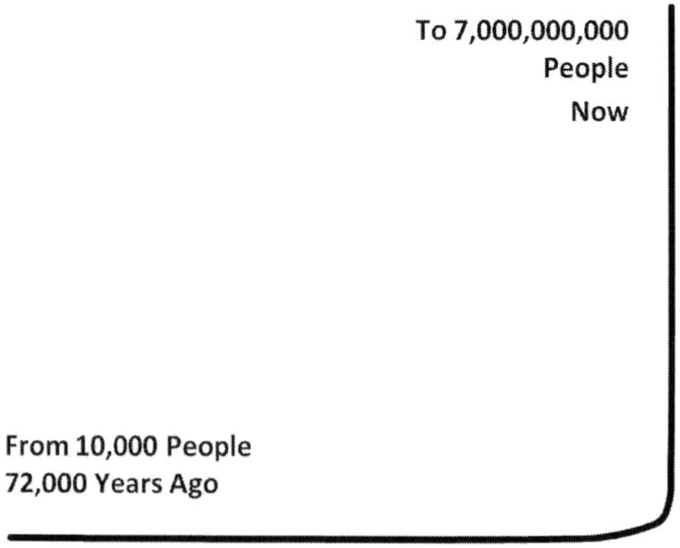

The Stranger Generator

To 7,000,000,000
People
Now

From 10,000 People
72,000 Years Ago

Figure 1: Then: Few - Now: Lots of Us

Humanity has exploded into the world.

A bottle neck occurred 72,000 years ago when Mount Toba erupted. The human population may have decreased to a tiny 1,000 to 10,000 in southern Africa. A large tribal clan's worth of us.

We slowly recovered up to maybe 10,000,000 people by 10,000 years ago when agriculture kicked in.

With the invention of cities we began a much faster expansion about 5,000 years ago.

By the time of Isaac Newton – the mid 1600s – we had reached about 500,000,000 folks.

Since then we have rapidly burst up to a swarm of about 7,000,000,000 of us humans around now.

Memorized Environment

It probably took 21 years to memorize our entire savanna environment. While brain and mind expanded.

About 1,000 square miles full of information: geographic milestones – animals that were big enough to kill us humans, prey that we needed for food – plants that could be gathered to eat, some dangerous. All humans needed "danger information" plus survival skills and knowledge.

It was critical to know a mind-full before you were able to function as an adult. Memorizing the environment in detail may have been among the reasons our brain expanded to 4 times its size over the last 2,500,000 years. Ice Ages may have helped with cycles of tough then easy life struggles.

We probably knew each predator, by name, with the size, strength, and speed to defeat us. Over 21 years of maturing we would have seen our human adult mentors defeat 2 or 3 generations of those predators with a known personality. We may have intimidated new born predators who would remember to be wary of us into adulthood.

We would have learned what kind of finagle was appropriate – the middle ground between fight and flight. A tactic somewhere in the wide center – not at the edges. Our expanding brain gave us multiple choices when we were confronted... fight – flight – or finagle – likely a bluff. Quick decisions by a supple, agile brain and its contents.

Overwhelming Complexity

Simplicity is frozen complexity - complexity is boiled simplicity.

A problem with American democracy is: cultural complexity is too great for anyone to understand. Bi-polar conflict analysis is a simplified way to think and to vote. Citizens may resist reasoning through the multiple cascading outcome contingencies of interlocked issues. So the default mind-stance is to depend on media highlights of surface issues - the simple ones that easy-trigger emotions.

Simplicity: compresses. Complexity: expands. Tension grows between the simple and the complex. Issues overlap in many haphazard ways - yet press toward 2-way polarity.

Each mind has an individual ability to address the spectrum from simple to complex. In complex surroundings how do we lace into creativity? Environments now revolve so fast that each human generation does not have time to digest the churn of lessons. The future has no true planning - only sub-optimized shaping to fit today's complexity.

Bi-polar short-term decisions on multi-polar long-term issues.

Vertical Education

All the 4 year olds and above would play together to become adults. The older children helped the younger learn and even kept them safe. With all the adults near bye to lend a hand if needed.

The advantage was that the children learned how to learn better by teaching as they aged.

When they were old enough they were "graduated" into being a life-long learning and teaching adult with a gentle long-term natural transition from being a toddler. They became excellent knowledge brokers.

Figure 2 shows a child in a vertical system with all the others in a gathering hunting band. Graceful mutual learners ratio.

Figure 2: A
Child Amidst
Vertical
Knowledge
Riches

Horizontal Education

Often starting very early a Civilized baby may be placed in day care. With a ratio of about 6 babies to 1 distracted care-giver. The child is in a one year cohort group with other same-age children.

Little of the gathering hunting band cooperative child learning dynamic.

The process continues through preschool, nursery school, kindergarten, elementary school, middle or junior high school, preparatory or high school, college, graduate school.

The same like-aged competitive cohorts. Easier on the formal educational system. Harder on the person.

Pumping out "factors of production" for the Industrial Revolution processing system.

Figure 3 shows a child in a horizontal system with about 30 others. Awkward teacher student ratio. No olders teaching the youngers.

Figure 3: Modern Class, All Same Age, Horizontal

Equality

Everyone in the gathering hunting band was equal. All shared equally in everything – most importantly the survival result.

Everyone carried their weight.

No place for marginal participation.

No place for inaction.

No place for second-class habits.

Every woman and every man was a full scale person.

No need for self-esteem. No need for self-loathing.

No need for self-respect. No need for self-disrespect.

No need for self-reliance.

No need for humility.

No need for arrogance.

Nothing but equals.

No jealousy. No envy.

A need for mutual cooperation. All the time.

Preferred

In Civilization the scramble is for preferred treatment. To be face-famous. To be money-rich. To be manipulation-powerful.

Often feigned humility or masked arrogance are used as manipulation tools - aimed at controlling other humans.

Perhaps the fundamental motivation is to find a way to be known by all - except now it is not the 600 in the ancient tribal clan.

The fame-goal today is a larger number from the human swarm - maybe millions - or billions.

Often disconnected by the electronic isolation of virtual anti-social networks - one dimensional with no real touching.

The bigger number can help support the rich or
famous - with the empowerment of preferred
treatment. Always expected through the habits
of the lucky-chance "rich" recipient. With
dollars or fame - through many expanding
apparent channels of physical or psychic
income.

Free-Range

Our ancestors were free – to roam anywhere.

No property lines to cross. No concept of land ownership. No concept of owning any physical thing.

The land was as free as the sky, or the air, or the sea.

My life had a "Free-Range" existence for the first 7 years of life. Am I typical for that heritage process? Of course not! I only have a gentle feel for what it must have been like. My mother had an instinct for how to raise a free-range child – with a nod toward Civilization.

How many generations would it take a human to genetically modify, through punctuated equilibrium, from a "Free-Range" primitive into a specialized, civilized person?

My sense is we haven't had time. We are still genetically close to "Free-Range."

Caged

The Civilized world is caged, constrained,
restricted, regulated - with many
indoctrinated habit chains crossing and
closing the mind. Habits that prevent free-
thought in an open mind. Habits defining a
specific culture. Habits define groups.
Habits define the groups you belong to.
Habits define you.

```
Habit patterns are the bars of the cage.

Culture imbeds a set of target habits in the
young, or the old if new to a culture.

We follow the habits and as they are repeated
- deep tracks channel the brain, it becomes
hard to conceive of things being any other way
than "our way."

Our culture - our group - me.

We are the right way to be.

The right way to live.

Leave us alone.

Let us go on as we are.
```

It was About "Us" – All the Time

In Primalization "togetherness" was carried to an extreme by modern standards. We slept together in the Group of 40. We ate together. We peed and pooped without embarrassment – without decorum. We did everything within sight of each other. Any other life style would have been suicidal for an individual. Our strength was us, together. To be alone on the savanna was an invitation to become food.

No one could hold back. You did all you could for the group.

There were few marginal performers. Everyone pitched in when needed.

```
     It's About "Me" - Most Times
Since the city.  Since Civilization.  The
change is clear.

Isolation - insulation - individualization.
Away from the group.  Sleeping alone in "your
own room."  Cast out of the home at 18 - "to
find your way in the world."
```

Building an individual culture. A "you" that
is alone. With a separate micro-culture –
with some loose connections to others – often
in groups that meet rarely.

How can life be about anyone other than you?
Attachments are weak.

As a child you are out of the home, away from
mom, soon after you are born. The day care
center, the nursery school, the pre-school,
the kindergarten.

Then its off to elementary school, Sunday
school, Scouts, dance lessons, music lessons,
sports, shows – often in a selection of remote
sites as your folks take on new adult duties –
in new places, with new people.

Then high school, college, graduate school –
maybe a fraternity or sorority. Lots of loose
attachments. The large number of
"connections" weakens then all.

Then you get a job, marry, have children –
perhaps divorce, maybe many times. Trying to
find at least one "other" that you resonate
with. No wonder "you" become the center of
your interest – your universe. What's the
option?

The really rich have compounds. Keep the kids
and grand-kids close – in a nuclear family
gathering hunting band, primal, together –
with remembered lessons fresh from the elders.
In a territory.

Chapter 5 – Years – Numbers – Mom

Sea Level to 6,000 Feet

Over the last 11,000,000 years the part of Africa our ancestors called home rose up 6,000 feet. A little more than a foot every 2,000 years.

We surfed on the East Side of the Great Rift as Africa bumped up against Eurasia. We did a figurative "hang-ten" – as tectonic plates created a super slow-motion wave crest.

New species were created as the environment changed. Old species changed to fit into the new co-evolution pattern.

What was once sea level jungle changed, to mile-high savanna. Our home lifted up under us. The trees left us – the rain water for them stayed at the lower sea level jungle.

We became who we are now – the most modern humans.

Some guess at 200,000 years ago.

Below Sea Level to the Moon

With Civilization came the ability to use tools to take us many places.

We can work at the bottom of the ocean. We have gone to the Moon – and come back.

Our first "space suits" were the clothes we wore to move into colder climates. The idea of clothing was important – garments were a tool that gave us a sense of geographic adventure. To divest – by moving part of the clan to the next valley when our birth valley got too crowded.

We now live on the mountains, in the desert, on the water, in the ocean.

High places. Low places.

Tough places. Easy places, usually flat.

Almost any place – humans call it "home."

Home on the range.

Home off the range.

Huts. Houses. Ships. Tents. Sleeping Bags. Grates. Apartments. Park Benches. Trailers. House Boats. Hotels. Barracks. Dormitories. Space Capsules. RVs. Condos. Caves. Cottages. Mansions. Homeless.

5,000,000 Years – Plus

For 5,000,000 years we lived as a cascade of changing human-like species among hunter-killer cats. We were below them in the apparent food chain – cat-food. Yet we were not killed away into extinction as a human race.

We prevailed: to turn the world of the cat inside out. Taming and shrinking them – or executing to extinction. The case of the saber-toothed tiger, perhaps by killing our common prey – or by forcing the biggest cats into closed, quarantined, marginal territory.

We stayed alive in a harsh, hostile, changing environment. For a very long time by modern human standards. Enough time for about 250,000 generations.

That's enough to over-fill a couple of Rose Bowls – with a single person representing each generation.

10,000 Years or Less

That long duration in a gathering hunting paradigm takes us to the today of the last

10,000 years. The time when Civilization begins to erupt. Since then we have diverged.

We expanded agriculture for about 5,000 years, in hamlets, villages, towns – before the next jump. Slowly increasing the density of our living.

We merged about 10 of our normal gathering hunting tribal clans to live in cities 5,000 years ago: the last mutual coherence of "natural" genes and "nurtured" culture.

About 5,000 humans habitually living in one small place is what we invented ourselves into, the first ancient cities.

Gradually the stress caused by differences in DNA-genetic response and cultural mind-interpretation increased.

In our generation of numbness we don't have the time to feel the rhythms of the 500 generations that trace our ancestors since the beginnings of agriculture, or the 250 since "the city" started.

Yet each generation made fundamental survival decisions that persist in the cultural map we inherit.

The decisions made within a generation were about how that generation coped, not about us – unseen in the distant future.

Still feels that way. The present generation seems unable to consider the next: when a decision is finally made.

600 People Tribal Clan

The gathering hunting person kept all that was needed in the mind, in the individual, and in the 40 person gathering hunting band – necessary working information. Institutional memory lived in the collective-mind of the 600 person tribal clan. We did it all ourselves without an external physical tool, inside our own minds. A distributed data base in the band with clan back-up redundancy.

Gathering-hunting tribal-clans – 600 people – thrived as generalists. A "then" gathering hunting tribal clan was about 600 people – about 15 bands -150 women, 150 men, 300 children. Figure 4 shows the "you" among 40, among 600.

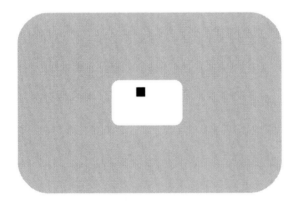

*Figure 4: You Among a Band of 40
and Tribal Clan of 600*

7,000,000,000 Hyper-Swarm

From strong bonds connecting to 600 people to faint, weak bonds to many more – now a possible 7,000,000,000 in total.

The tribal clan of 600 was always "together" in about 1000 square miles. A confusing neighborhood to the folks of today. Now you might live within 100 feet of 600 people and not know any. Individuals can be flitting in and out of cubbyhole homes with little of your notice.

Many civilized associations are superficial connections. Most of humanity is beyond personal knowledge. How can you relate to them all? The 600 was knowable – the 7,000,000,000 is not.

So many options: science, judgment, calculation, humility, art, emotion, instinct, self-expression, alone – an audience. Primalization connection was always strong among the life-time 600. The basis for 6 degrees of separation. In Civilization we have an unknown number of shallow connections. Yet still an emotional need for a strong 600.

Think Globally – 7,000,000,000 People in the world hyper-tribe.

Act Locally – 600 People in your equivalent modern tribe. Muddled in the middle – where most policy lies.

Figure 5 gives a size comparison of "you" in an eroding gathering hunting band imbedded in an early ancient city of 5,000.

*Figure 5: You Among the 40,
Among the 600, In a City of
5,000.*

It isn't possible to show a graphic to highlight a diminished you in the population of the United States – 1 out of 310,000,000. About 500,000 tribes.

Or in the World population – 1 out of 7,000,000,000. About 10,000,000 tribes.

Population matters to the relative "you."

Unified Mostly Active Life

The Group of 40 was active. Finding something to eat in the most likely places – with no ability to store for later. Searching the surroundings for danger. Selecting: fight – flight – or finagle when the response to danger was needed. Walking a lot – from the night's sleep in a safe place – to a place to eat – and on to another safe place.

While doing all of it together.

Lots of muscles being used. With just enough food. Just enough energy.

Lots of eye focusing. Lots of active thinking.

Lots of action. A fitness life style.

Segmented Mostly Passive Life

Maybe you eat breakfast with someone – more likely alone. Commute in your car probably alone. Perhaps wait at the bus stop – or on the subway platform. Maybe ride your bike – alone. People all around – usually part of the stranger swarm.

Work with associates. Or go to school with classmates. More segments. Move as an individual to the next class of strangers.

Living in a city with a grid of streets, linear, in squares. Riding with strangers in an elevator.

Dwelling in rooms that are linear boxes, maybe with linear grid ceilings. Straight lines everywhere. Segmenting the space. Each space with different people.

In cars, on buses, crowded into air planes, standing on the subway – no need to carry much. Not much exercise.

During the day, fixed focal length staring. In a room, at a computer screen. At night staring at a television or a PC monitor. Maybe a book.

At least the book gives the imagination a chance to dance in the mind. Creating mental images, imagination-intense.

The most passive is television - supplying both sight and sound. With some action but all at the same focal length, so the mind knows it can go into an even more passive state. The brain knows on-screen action is not real.

No muscles to move. No real decisions to be made. Too passive. Too segmented.

Nomadic

In Primalization we roamed our territory – perhaps about 1,000 square miles of East African savanna near the Equator.

We did not have a permanent camp.

We may have spent a few days in one place. But we would soon be gone to another.

Possibly the safe place to sleep was a long walk from the best place to get food.

We responded to our needs.

As our gathering hunting band wandered we would come across other bands from the same tribal clan. They would be our friends and relatives – not enemies.

Cooperation among those like us. To compete with other living things to continue to live. To create a network of co-evolution.

Anchored

In Civilization we are anchored to our property, with our tools, with our work, with our things: houses, cars, furniture, books.

With our culture – and by the wants generated in an over-crowded stranger-rich planet. With a temporary rich resource base for technology to play.

Wants start as gentle constraints but shift into hard needs: clothes, fashion, education, entertainment, class, money, recreation, expectation, intention.

Somewhere buried deep within the wants that culture has crafted for us: nestle our real, "true?" – needs.

In tough times it is the muscle of need that requires satisfaction – not the spangle, the bling, of want.

We see that happening after hurricanes, earthquakes, volcanoes, and tsunamis.

That's when the artificial anchors of Civilization are pulled up.

Fundamentals again become critical and basic – until forgotten after ease sets in.

Life or death issues lost.

Intense "Mother-Love"

A primitive baby may have spent 90% of the day in skin contact with Mom. The only non-contact was when they were asleep and not touching by chance. As a toddler the child was walking – still in skin contact – hand in hand. Or carried sometimes – asleep in Mom's arms.

The child had a couple of decades to move slowly through a range of life experience, and play at being an adult, to finally become full grown. To memorize the environment.

You can remember all that you really need to know.

Confused "Care-Giver-Like"

A modern baby still picks up on the intense love broadcast from Mother. Yet it is not there all the time. A succession of insulating non-connected care-givers are interspersed among real Mom-time.

In day care, nursery school, with nannies. The infant perceives a discounting of mother-love toned down to "like." Intense love may not be learned by a baby when the brain has maxi-plasticity and hyper-learning is possible. Those first 18 critical months of new life.

Mother-love is not there all the time, Mom isn't there.

It is hard to be a 24/7 mom in an 8 to 5 professional world. Income from both Mom and Dad is needed for a target life style.

There is no direct substitute for a Mother, although the baby's aunts may be very close. They would have been there in the gathering hunting band.

They would have a very close scent.

Probably picked up by the baby before the sense of smell gets dulled by the confused odors of Civilization.

Sane

Our Primal fore-bearers were subject to the normal stress of prey-predator living – dangerous, deadly, expected.

The brain and its contents, the mind, developed over many millions of years. The stress it felt was not only normal, but perhaps a reason for our spectacular brain growth: 4 times the size in 2,500,000 years!

Sanity within our great mind is our birthright.

Insane

In Civilization are we all crazy?

The environment is not stable – it is hyper-dynamic, changing moment by moment in fundamental ways.

Technology changes more in one day now than it did in many generations before us.

Cultures around the world have grown differently, different plants, different animals, different climate, different terrain – all creating fundamentally different approaches to how humans live.

Now cultures are all jumbling with accelerating technology. Pockets of culture are now grab bags.

No one can understand the over-arching human hyper-culture. No one can resist the stress of sudden constant change.

We all do the best we can with our own brand of dealing – crafting a "normal" setting for our own simulation of sanity.

Recognize that you and all around you are "abnormal in the mind." You are not gathering and hunting in the million-year sense.

You are using genetic skills that have been overloaded with hundreds of generations of cultural change – building habits to match. Each generation making changes needed for its own many purposes.

Now make the best of it.

You are still a gatherer hunter underneath
your habits. As you get older: life
experience finds clues about who you really
are – continuously transforming, always with
new experiences.

Perhaps becoming the ever wiser elder.

Rich in experience, scarred, yet surviving
"your way."

The Primal life behind the Civilized mask.

Chapter 6 – Elders – Chance – Wilderness

Slowly Acquired Wisdom of the Elders

Over a lifetime of gathering and hunting an elder gains wisdom, another way of saying "experience." Each yearly experience was built upon the years before – with very little change in the environment or the human culture.

It was just a part of life to be known by all 600 in your gathering hunting tribal clan – and to be recognized as a clan-wide elder when you had lived a long life.

You had wisdom tempered through a series of dangerous adventures retold as stories.

You lived them. Remembered them. And could express them. If you were old you were wise by default.

Story was fundamental to wisdom.

Quick Celebrity Status Lust

Today's world seems to want quick celebrity – not based on experience and wisdom but technology and luck. The lust for celebrity may reflect the natural need to be known by all the "humanity of the day": only 600 in the distant past – now 7,000,000,000.

Yet the hyper-tribe can not be very well known. Too big. Too many. Too non-local. Too specialty scattered.

Stories are still told. To entertain. To teach.

Some truth – some fiction – some pure imagination.

```
Only now the stories come from screen writers
and book authors and playwrights and reporters
and public relations story makers.

The stories come at us now not metered by age,
but apparent random, to any audience that has
access to: television, personal computer, or
any number of quick-invention electronic
gadgets, with iBling.

Our children now are mentored by a matrix of
unstructured fiction that shapes their world
view.  Only a few true stories are now told on
Grandma or Grandpa's knee.

Many celebrities achieve status based mostly
on roles-played.  Sometimes fame is founded on
the carefully crafted notoriety of fictional
"real" lives.
```

All Leaders & All Followers

Every adult in the gathering hunting band was ready to lead or to follow at an instant's notice, whichever fit the immediate survival need. If you were at the point of action in a dangerous episode – you took over.

Each person was a follower-leader depending on the need.

Maybe 80-20, 80 percent follower and 20 percent leader.

The leadership function could not rest with a single individual.

The risk of loosing any one person as the only leader would be too great. And the need for episodic leadership too unexpected in both time and place.

The elders would have been respected and acknowledged for their wisdom and advice in quiet times – consultants. The youngsters would have dealt with high energy, immediate action – right beside the oldsters.

Narrow Short-Range Leaders

Now we have leaders with short-range vision who achieve a "position" and all below them are followers, most of the time – with little exception. This is disheartening to any adult human. We instinctively expect to be equals and expect to have leadership responsibility – sometimes.

What would it be like to be on an assembly line for a lifetime? To be valued, specifically, for your hands – a part of the body, not even the whole you. To be "a hand."

With short-range vision, only the near, the obvious, the now, the new – is considered with any clarity, and only for the current stream of immediate moments.

The distant future, the far place, develops through chance without much vision. "Now" trumps "when."

In the Primal era the later-time of "when" didn't matter much, it would be about the same. In Civilization everything changes.

Even leaders, who are considered good, will often bluff to maintain their "position."

Aimed short-range finagling, with some luck – to remain in power.

Examples are many in politics, business, sports, entertainment.

Kingdom of Probability

In Primalization probability was all around us. We had little ability to change our luck. We lived in a consistent territory of uncertainty.

Risk and risk avoidance was always with us. Clear and obvious. There was no security force except the gathering hunting band itself.

Domains of Chance

In Civilization we are able to shift and move into different domains of chance. We "push our luck" by decisions we make — the navigated personal directions we take.

Plus there is larger luck.

Luck is layered. The ancestors you had. The parents who met and created you. The cradle nurturance you had. The country you were in. The surrounding "big religion." The language you speak. The friends you found. The schools you attended. The jobs you selected and could get.

Plus the luck of not reaching some of the milestones that human genes expect, to become a fully functioning adult human.

Many decisions have moved you along a cascade of domains of chance. You can prepare yourself to play in the lottery, yet what actually happens has a large component of chance, luck, probability, uncertainty, risk. You can do some guiding while recognizing when a lucky break happens, a component in your life lottery.

Suppose you hadn't met a particular person at a specific time, at a certain place? Life follows risks and flows.

Perhaps a lot like chaos theory, with strange attractors and bifurcations.

There will always be a few spectacular lottery winners.

The "very successful" in Civilization's fame and fortune sweepstakes are in that status by chance. Yet they, and the culture, much prefer a story based on merit. A reasoned-oriented notoriety is more palatable, perhaps "I" have a chance to get there by carefully crafted chance-free decisions.

"Luck favors the prepared."

Yet the preparation is also luck-based.

One lucky break after another – a panorama of cascading chance. Some good. Some bad. All a part of living in an uncertain World.

Outside

The savanna was outside. Mostly grass – some trees – some water holes and streams, all outside. That's where we were during the day.   Maybe we slept in a cave at night on the crumbling edge of the Great Rift. With lots of walking every day – from a night-time refuge to day-time food with plenty of water – and back again.

Lots of walking. Commuting from a safe place to sleep to a good place to eat.

With natural exercise along the way.   Some adventure. Considerable danger. Exertion to keep fit, automatically – part of a life style of balanced fitness.

Memorizing each change in the radius of environment, and gauging what might be between you and the landscape edge. "Vision" comes from eye-probing the horizon.

Inside

Now our time is spent mostly inside. Away from the sun and the breeze. Mostly riding from one indoor site to another, in cars, in buses, in planes – in subways, twice removed, in a train under ground.

Little walking. Some access to gym equipment – put to use once in awhile.

Sitting in pre-positioned chairs. Not getting the muscle fitness of just squatting when you want to stop and rest: on a savanna with no place to sit.

Not moving much, watching electronic screens. Making use of labor-saving devices, fashionable muscle-wasting inventions. Away from millions of years of partnership with a natural environment.

Now living for days without seeing anything exterior except a carefully crafted "outside" of mowed grass, planted trees, constructed buildings, graded roads with curbs to tame the rain water runoff. Wildness – the wilderness – a long way from nature.

So far away it is seldom visited. Seldom enjoyed for the peace, the solitude, the lack of crowding strangers, non-time bound.

Enjoyment often implies: a portable TV, a cell phone or a smart phone, plus a Geographic Positioning System, no map.   Ah Wilderness.

One-Day-at-a-Time

In our ancient world we lived one-day-at-a-time.

There was little to plan for, the future was going to just happen and be a lot like the past.

There were lessons learned from the past, repeated with little variation – and mind sharpening through repetition.

We reacted to the slow-motion co-evolution happening around us, responding to weather, responding to nature.

Reaction was our natural response.

Reaction at the time of a challenge or an opportunity. Not becoming prey or a casualty to a natural disaster. Or finding something to eat, or a safe place to sleep.

None-Day-at-a-Time

Now its "None-Day-at-a-Time" – usually decoupled from direct natural consequences.

We try to plan – still mostly for the short range future.

We try to learn from the past – which is nowhere like the present.

What's past is an uncertain prologue.

We live in a continuing shift of culture – with technology creating tools much faster than they can be digested.

We bounce from one idea, to the next concept, to another optional gadget.

Time – Places – People – Things – Ideas – Processes – shifting and moving, as we swim in the stress of uncertainty.

Natural disasters do happen. Unplanned for, though we know they will come.

Yet much of our time awareness comes from human-made considerations.

The project is due on June 30th. Taxes need to be paid on the 15th of April. The fiscal year ends on the 30th of September.

The commuter bus comes at 6:45 am. The final report for my class is due Friday.

Time dancing to the whims of humanity.

Except, of course, your birthday - a natural event worthy of celebration.

Wilderness

We lived in the wild.

Surrounded by wild things – some trying to kill us for food.

All known.

We lived where we had intimate knowledge of all that surrounded us.

Dangerous but known.

Urban

The cultural setting now is built up, architecture, landscaping. Much is man-created, little left to nature - nothing we can touch is deep wild.

We get some protection from the created city-wild with police, fire protection, and the military.

Our lives are lived in a city-inspired simulation, virtual, designed.

Much of it crafted by early generations. Each
with its own idea on what resources humanity
should use to continue in life. Each
generation intent on their own time and place.

With little regard for the generations to
come.

Leaving ever less stocks of resources to
assemble into new solutions.

The urban environment creates different
dangers, many hidden, many stealthy. Products
of Civilization: Hamlets, towns, villages,
cities, suburbs, disturbia.

Over 3,500,000,000 people now live in urban
places around the World. We recently went
beyond half of us swarming in cities.

From zero only 5,000 years ago.

Light Weight

Early humans were light on the environment.

So few people that the simple things they did would be easily absorbed, covered, gone soon. No "waste."

What we ate and drank was used by the body for fuel – and then was returned to nature. Quickly absorbed.

No pollution.

Nothing needed to be self-consciously recycled.

Heavy

We get ever heavier. Our footprints don't
vanish with the wind.

We are inventing, consuming rare resources,
building to last, growing in population,

tossing many things into a slow-to-heal environment.

Our markings are hard to erase. The wind only scatters.

The oceans carry the things that float to the swirl at the very center, some sink. With what effect on the sea bottom?

We expel things into the air. Without any knowledge of what might happen.

And when we consider what might happen we think in short-term straight lines.

Some things can have linear trends for a long time by human standards.

Then a knee threshold happens - a hockey stick curve. The things that shape us can suddenly go off in many directions - at unknown speeds.

That's the real danger in climate change.

We don't have any idea where the thresholds are, or how much we effect them.

Our heavy footprints may be trampling out a vintage where the true grapes of wrath are stored.

Ready to pounce.

Humans doing heavy clog dancing with no real knowledge of the slant on the dance floor.

Chapter 7 – Truth – Trust – Savanna

Truth

Since we were all in contact most of the time – we all had nearly the same experiences.

We knew what happened in any life chapter. With the same view – usually seen from less than 50-feet away.

There was no need for guile among humans.

We did need to be full of stealth to hunt – we needed every trick in the book to kill animals that did not want to be killed.

We could decoy. We could falsify to attract, to lure, to seem safe – with animals. And to not become prey ourselves.

Yet with other humans only the truth.

Without property, without things, without land title, there was little room for festering envy or hidden jealousy or false status.

Mental Manipulation

We don't hunt other animals to kill them in the general culture. So that brand of non-human manipulation doesn't occur much now.

At present the manipulation, the finagle, has taken a different focus. We manipulate each other with shadings of the truth. We might withhold critical facts. We might simply tell untruths. Or our studied, advantageous, version of "the truth." Could be we are silent when we should talk.

Advertising attempts to convert a want into a need, ending in a decision to purchase. Does advertising slant?

We are subject to entertainment scripts that try to grab our attention, sometimes with fantasy, always for a purpose. A purpose for who?

Perhaps the role of any fiction is to give counterbalance to our stressed lives. With elements in entertainment that simulate the dangers we had in Primalization as prey. Maybe providing a simulated virtual gathering hunting group to connect with too.

"Political Correctness" seems to be when the other side has a clash with our alternate speculations on correctness.

In books, at work, with strangers. Lots of attempted manipulations of the mind. To help negotiate among our personal micro-cultures.

Balance-Brained

To survive on the savanna we needed everything working at full capacity – available on demand.

That meant we needed to think linearly with the left hemisphere of the brain and randomly with the right hemisphere, whenever it was appropriate. When needed.

Our thought processes were balance-brained.

During our time on the savanna we went through a long developmental cycle of foraging – gathering easier to get food. Then scavenging – gathering killed food from the hunting success of another species. Finally, with the right tool weapons, we began to hunt. Killing animals ourselves.

We needed a fully functioning brain to do that, to allow the progression to hunter.

Linear Left-Brained

Now we are in a linear world. With visual lines all around us. Everywhere we look.

Linearity in our culture, in many ways: language, deadlines, roads, appointments at a specific time on a calendar day. Time awareness minute to clock minute. Space awareness in a flurry of map grids.

We live a rigid linear thinking-style most of the time.

The left-hemisphere becomes more dominant, the "science" part. Data to be cared for. Repeatable. Endorsed and verified by others. Pushing to be perfect.

The random right-hemisphere becomes less used – the "art" part. The spiritual part. One-of-a-kind solutions. Creative. Done most likely alone. Untrainable.

Bombarded with time, space, and idea linearity. Feeding and forming the left brain.

But the right brain still won't be smothered. It still pops out.

Perhaps a well mixed recipe of emotions, intuition, 6th sense, random brain waves. Flashing into inspired creativity, dimensionless.

Trusting

We lived in a trusting climate among humans.

All was known. All could be trusted.

Trusting was a way of life. Trust among humans was survival.

Untrusting

"Who do you trust?"

Untrusting becomes a necessary component of any new modern contact between humans.

Even the shallow contact of the Internet where e-mail messages are phishing for people to scam.

The only place a human can be trusting is with those who have proven themselves to be trustworthy. Near. Known.

Always uncertain with a stranger.

No more "contracts with a handshake" - "my word is my bond."

With little animal hunting still happening. With so many human strangers. With the shift to competition as a spiritually confirmed way-of-life.

What have we done?

We have done a quick biological shift.

Humans now have become prey and predator on other humans, our own species.

The shifting prey-predator relationship among humans gets us resources. Predator one moment. Prey the next.

Prey and predator together in each of us helps control the rapid population growth of our species.

Trust but verify.

40-Mile Savanna Radius

Our range on the savanna would be about 40 miles in radius – perhaps 1000 square miles of territory.

Enough to provide food for all 600 of the tribe, as they walked from place to place in their gathering bands of 40.

That would be in about 15 bands – goal-wandering around a drainage basin valley. Self-tasked with finding food and water and rest and safety.

12,500 Mile Global Radius

Today we humans span the globe.

We live on all continents – with dozens of people wintering over on Antarctica.

Starting about 40,000 years ago we dispersed to fill the Earth.

By 10,000 years ago we were spread out from Africa to the tip of South America.

We covered the world in a migration of about 30,000 miles in about 30,000 years – about a mile per year.

Most of us are aware of the presence of others all around the globe.

We know our collective home is a sphere planet – with lots of limits.

We have taken all the big species niches and made them our own.

The very tiny are another story.

The microbes and viruses are still out there – along with insects.

We don't do well with sharing so we are after
them too.

They fight back: the germs and the bugs.

Savanna Geography

The savanna geography was flat – mostly grass – with isolated
trees and some bushes.

With the Great Rift, or any discontinuity, offering a night-time
place-of-refuge from our natural enemies. The hunting animals
that wanted us for food.

Usually there were near bye herds of easier-to-get prey.

Animals that were naturally fleet, but with a few slow pokes to
feed the big predators.

Over millions of years as the savanna rose up the jungle left us.
Only a few trees and bushes survived along water courses.
Over a mile below in the Congo River basin the moisture still
fell and the jungle still thrived.

The change was slow enough for us to adjust: walking on 2
legs, binocular color vision, large brain, multipurpose digestive
system, a variety of teeth types, mostly hairless.

Many Geographies

We live in every kind of terrain – from sea-
level to over 10,000 feet in the mountains.

In swamp land and desert.

Some of our species have even left the earth
for months at a time to go into orbit – or for
days on the Moon.

Humans have walked the Moon geography.

We build cities on river flood plains, and
wonder why they flood.

We build cities on earthquake faults, and wonder why they shake apart.

We build cities near ocean beaches, and wonder why they are inundated by tidal waves.

Nature is indifferent to what we do, or where we live, or why we live there.

Natural will do whatever its many forces want with the continents that we drift around upon.

Unified Culture

For perhaps 5,000,000 years we had a series of unified cultures. Each culture helping its own grouped human-like species to survive. With the culture and its living members slowly changing to match the slowness of change in the natural environment.

With a connected cascade that would survive enough so that we are here now. In the human culture and human shape we recognize.

Until 10,000 years ago a gathering hunting human culture was covering all the world.

With minor differences because of climate, altitude, attitude, plants, animals, water, sun angle.

Personal Micro Cultures

Now in the developed world we have many choices: what religion to follow, what education to gather, what job to do, who we should raise a family with, where we should live, when we should travel, who we should befriend, how we should live.

The result is that we are all different.

Each of us has a unique background with a
personal pattern and pacing of experiences.

It makes collective decision making hard.
Each view point on any issue can have basic,
sometimes unvoiced, differences. Critical
connections may appear strong yet are weak.
We are surround by clustered meta-cultures
composed from many linked individual personal
micro-cultures.

A rich human mixture of personal speculations.
Each speculator owed her and his equal due.

Each speculation has a strength phased among
the textures of assumptions, beliefs, ideas.
Sometimes conflicted understandings occupy the
same mind at different times.

The relative courage of any conviction is
often determined by the context of expression.

Reactive

Our usual style of life was to react to what was happening
around us.

Respond to danger. Take advantage of some chance plants to
gather.

Walk to a place to get water. Scavenge the kill of a predator
who had a full belly. Hunt and kill prey unlucky enough to be
in our range. Stay away from hungry predators. Stay away
from actively smoking volcanoes.

The environment was changing around us in slow motion and
we reacted to those changes. With rapid spiked changes to
respond to – occasionally. Tectonic plates move as fast as a
fingernail grows, yet build to a sudden earthquake.

Proactive

We now take proaction.

We randomly change the environment.

We farm land.

We build houses.

We erect shopping centers.

We construct damns.

We burn fuels.

We stock animals.

We drive cars.

We fly planes.

We operate computers.

We create countries.

We make contracts.

We work in offices. We work out in gyms.

We keep trying to change the human habitat "for the better" –

With "for the worse" results.

We have temporary wisdom that sees a "problem" and then "solves" it with a solution that seems sweet yet eventually turns sour.

It is hard to find even a temporary steady state while being knee-jerk proactive.

Technology is multi-edged, cutting in many directions.

Thus, political policy is tough to do.

Roger Gilbertson

Chapter 8 – Real – Play – Is

Real

Our ancient life was real. It had a texture and a tone that could be felt.

We got real experience.

With some story telling when a hunting party returned. The hunters needed to share the news of dangers met and solved. Negative tales with a positive punch line – survival.

Stories of the gather were equally important. Where were the best plants. Which plants were poisonous, which were medicinal.

Some stories had to be funny. Funny feels so human. Laughing as release, as entertainment.

Maybe the reason we laugh today – the joy of survival after uncertainty. Comedians understand.

Virtual

Civilization feels like a game, a virtual experiment that involves the entire human race, everyone on the planet.

With no control group.

Each separate culture, each country's political philosophy, each religion, each neighborhood, each family has its own virtual content. Shared myths.

We start learning special content, perhaps before we are born, and are indoctrinated by the time we become an adult.

It still takes about 21 years to become a
physical adult, perhaps we never can become a
cultural adult - too much rapid change.

Maybe by 42? What about 63? Or 84?

Perhaps the only reality foundation today is
the time spent in the womb - with mother.
Every human starts with 9 months in
Primalization.

After our zero birthday we are bombarded with
choices and imperatives, that indoctrinate us
into a modern range of cultures. The result
is our own personal, unique micro-culture.

Perhaps with membership in a strong group we
can get some feel for what it was like to be
in a single gathering band for a lifetime. At
least a touch.

Physical Closeness

The gathering hunting band was seldom apart, within easy reach proximity most of the time.

We walked, foraged, gathered, scavenged, hunted, slept, eliminated, all very close to each other. We had to stay close. Survival depended on the cohesion of the group.

Physical proximity was an important characteristic.

We had eye-contact connection.

We could see who we were communication with and they could see us. We had 3-D body language and all the 5 senses, maybe plus the intuitive 6th sense, with unskeptical clarity.

Humans had to watch each other closely for communication. We didn't start using a spoken language until 40,000 years ago.

Until then it was facial expression, stance, pace, posture, gesture, grunts, intuition. Maybe some ESP?

Electronic Isolation

Electronics have isolated us from personal contact since the Industrial Revolution matured into the Electronics Revolution.

The flood has been from telegraph to telephone to radio to television to personal computer to the World Wide Web to e-mail to text messaging to social networking.

Each innovation takes us further away from direct human contact.

Contacts now are loose, shallow, fleeting, with less solid meaning and many unclear, ambiguous messages.

Each relationship category, family, friend, associate, colleague is discounted.

Electrons in temporary high-tech lock-step are nowhere near as expressive as organic molecules doing an improvised folk dance.

Stable Group Dynamic

Our ancestors had lifetime stability in group dynamics. In the band most of the time. With the tribal clan some.

The Group of 40 and the Clan of 600 were rock solid.

All of humanity as far as anyone knew.

No strangers.

No specialists.

No economic surplus to scrap over.

The group dynamic was birth, life, death with an interesting journey along the way.

Maxi-Shift Dynamic

Humans in Civilized groups have a daily shifting dynamic. Being among other people you have known for awhile.

Then suddenly being isolated among a spectrum of strangers as you go elsewhere.

Bouncing among relatives, friends, colleagues, co-workers, associates, enemies, partial strangers, full strangers.

Accelerated by the Web where the physical is minimized. The real isn't there. The dimensions are abstracted, virtual, electronic.

Nothing there except some stampeding electrons. Corralled for a moment to make sense, until hurried off to a different polarity.

The frenzy of converting the findings of science into profitable tools and products continues, unabated.

Combine the hectic pace of technology and the bursting rate of the human population and the dynamic has chaotic dimensions.

Free Play to Generalist

The child of a gathering hunting band free-played at being an adult. It took 21 years to get there but the process that matured the young human honed the skills for adulthood.

Mistakes would be made. Some dangerous. Maybe lethal.

All the skills needed were present by the time of adulthood. The generalist child was ready for a full human life at about 21 years old.

Mother had a lot to do with it, in those earliest months of maxi-brain-plasticity. But later on the band was like a one-room school house. In the middle years of childhood you had about 20 other kids around you.

About one in each "year group." So you probably did not have any true age or grade cohorts. The older kids did a lot of the teaching – along with keeping you safe. Teaching for humans has become a way to learn more about the subject than the range of skills needed by the individual student.

As you got older the adults would phase in more to be sure you had the right skills. Mom phased over to the next baby in about 4 or 5 years. The band knew you and loved you.

Guided Education to Specialist

Today play is ever more restricted. Free-play is isolated into tiny random patches now and again.

No child left unregulated.

The child is too soon popped into the spectrum of: day care – nursery school – kindergarten – elementary school – middle school – prep school – college – grad school – job – retirement.

The indoctrination is to craft us to be an obedient factor of production. Sit down in your assigned seat when the whistle blows. Raise your hand to go to the bathroom. Raise your hand to ask a question. Go to lunch when the whistle blows. Go home when another whistle blows.

Do what you are told to do to fit a factory culture.

Select a specialty, or take the suggestion of someone else, and follow that skill path. Let other skills go, to wilt, to wither, by default.

By doing a specialty well you can make a living with it. Maybe the specialty will be there for your lifetime. Maybe you will get lucky and become a wealthy celebrity with power and credibility.

Much more likely you will be "regular."

Permanent Partners

In the savanna world, your territory, you knew everyone. You had permanent partners in a life of survival in a dangerous place. You helped everyone else survive. They helped you.

The 40 in your gathering hunting band.

The 600 in your gathering hunting tribal clan.

As far as you knew the whole human race was that 600.

Still the magic number for humans – 600.

Temporary Acquaintances

Now often the best we can do is have temporary friends, the people we pass by on the way to becoming an elder.

Some stay for months - others for years.

If we are truly lucky in Civilization we have some life-time friends.

They could be from the old neighborhood, or high school, or college, or the military - or anywhere. Where there was real sharing.

Often we remember the younger times more than the latest times. The younger friends more than the latest acquaintances. Many connections over a lifetime often discount the ones in later life.

Friendship can get lost in the shuffled cards of people.

It is possible to have new permanent friends at an advanced age, yet rarely. Dealing with strangers becomes a habit. You might ask for a person's name then promptly forget it.

Or ask for an email address and never use it. Business cards often vanish.

Although personal bookmarks may survive in a book — that's what I give out to memorable strangers — bookmarks.

If you have 10 true friends in a life-time, like the 10s group you would have known in a gathering hunting band, you are fortunate.

Continuous Eye Refocus

Outdoors, with wide horizons and close dangers, we would be continuously refocusing our eyes. Giving our brain a workout in pattern recognition and processes of thought.

We would search for unfolding events that demanded physical reaction. Making action stories from patterns.

Sometimes we would "chip the flint" to make tools, when we had young eyes. By the time we reached about 40 our ability to see things up close would fade.

Then as elders we would seek the horizon. Looking away from near detail toward far "vision."

Vision became both the reality and the living abstraction of the elder in thoughtful action.

Visioning to the horizon and perhaps envisioning over the horizon. The better to think and dispense wisdom.

Short Focus Stare

Today the eyes spend a lot of time with a short fixed-focus stare: at the TV screen, at the computer monitor, at the tail lights of the car ahead of you, at the movie screen, at the wall, across the street.

With few broad vistas.

If the brain doesn't have active work to do, like stroking the keyboard, it may think it's time to sleep. Go into a kind of coma, the logical result of too much passive long-session screen viewing.

Brain-eroding for anyone.

Disaster for small children. Their brain hyper-plasticity can mistake the inaction as expected adult reality.

Even if the screen seems to scream with dynamic change, the eye focus is still staring at the same point, passive. No real physical movement that might require a response with muscles.

Your mind knows its only pretend.

Television for children is a deadly baby sitter. Yet peer groups expect it.

Is

We lived in an "is" world.

That was the way it was.

"What you see is what you get."

Doses of reality.

No way to leave reality.

Where you sit is where you stand.

Fun, entertainment, recreation, built into the fabric of living.

Ought

Now we live in a forest of "oughts."

Things ought to be this way.

Things ought to be that way.

Things ought to be different.

Each the result of an individual's incremental speculations.

It is hard to get agreement.

It is hard to get an understanding of what today's "is" is.

The isolated individuals in today's culture can't readily agree on what is important and what is not. Or what the critical characteristics of life are.

It is hard to craft answers if the questions are maxi-fluid.

No wonder we wander through many possible solutions hoping something will help.

Economic stress is always interesting.

Commercial downturns usually get a name.

The Long Depression.

The Great Depression.

The Great Recession.

What ought we do? Maybe try another name.

Chapter 9 – Sharing – Policy – Numbers

24/7/365 Living with Intimates

We were together all the time in our gathering band, 24 hours a day,7 days a week, all through the year.

Every year we would have most weeks of intimate living with 40 people and a month or 2 in close contact with 600 people. Thus – 2 circles with 100 percent overlap – like a bull's eye.

Everyone knew everyone. Zero degrees of separation within the 600.

Work – Play – Live Separately

Life is now compartmentalized.

Each part of our life is played out in a separate location, often with different people for short, well-measured, lengths of time.

We may not have any friends from work.

Our family may not know our friends or work colleagues.

Our new friends don't know our old friends.

We may go to meetings where everyone is a stranger.

We become a linchpin that connects many abstracted circles of acquaintance, where only a few people among the total might know each other.

Even your family is dispersed in time and place.

Not one real gathering band – but many weak virtual gathering bands – with no tribal clan.

Six degrees of separation.

If each of your 600 each knew another 600 — you can see that in 6 jumps everyone in the world has weak access to everyone else.

A theoretical modern gathering hunting swarm of all the 7,000,000,000.

Now spread World-wide.

A modern super-sized biomass of large animals.

Always Eat Together

The gathering hunting band shared every meal.

Portion size would be equal.

We ate the same things together. Fruit, vegetables, leaves, roots, berries, nuts, bugs. Rarely some meat from animals and birds. Possibly some fish. Anything that we knew would give us food to live.

With the only balance based on what was available.

The men on a hunting episode might fill up on meat after a kill. Carrying some of the rest home for the others would have been easier that way. Unless the entire gathering band was near the hunt. Meat could not be saved. Once the kill was left behind scavengers would get it. It would spoil fast in our tropic territory.

At mealtime we could share in communications, continue to strengthen the bonds of connection. Highlight lessons learned when they were fresh.

Often Eat Alone

Today it is common for each member of a family to micro-wave their own personal meal — taken from the freezer. Nuc the cold stuff.

Then go off to their own personal TV, or DVD player, or PC, or video game, or iPad, or SmartPhone, or the latest electronic gadget. And eat alone with a concentration on impersonal individual "entertainment."

No intimate real connection with family and friends just abstract connection to scripts, authors, computer programmers, actors, musicians, advertisers, game programmers, whose true interest is elsewhere, remote, designed to create and attract a particular profit-oriented mind-space environment.

Angled to get more of the same addictive behavior ultimately to stimulate a decision to buy something.

Occasionally work groups will have lunch together.

Often the connection is only work, an incomplete, partial dimension. Anything personal is just on the surface.

Sharing

Everything was shared. There was no property.

No personal property.

No real estate.

Only each other – together on the savanna.

Complete sharing.

Selfish

Now ideas of property and ownership have intruded.

The grandest goal seems to acquire, to own, as much as you can.

Boundaries. Fences. Contracts. Locks. Clutter.

Too many books, yet books are really store houses of ideas, perhaps a special category. Books don't need electronics to work.

Patents turn ideas into property. Even though the idea has been around for a long time in a slightly different form.

Copyright converts written concepts into property.

Trademarks translate art into property.

Real estate location converts fresh air into property. If you live close to the Pacific Ocean in Los Angeles some of your real estate value comes in with the off-shore breeze.

Property, acquired, hoarded, seldom shared.

Often highlighted and proudly shown to prove "success." A museum to the power of purchase.

Donated after the show value goes down, to get some emotional feeling of what sharing was in the gathering hunting group.

Proofs of acquisition skill are all around us, a demonstration of entrepreneurial consumption.

Everything Used Up

With a nomadic life, and no pockets, or even clothes. There was nothing worth carrying except babies. If we found or made a simple tool it was temporary. We could make or find another for the next use.

Toss it.

The woven basket, and clothes, are about 40,000 years old. About the time we started carrying things.

When we started transporting we could keep some few things. A favorite tool. Perhaps something felt just right or that just looked "nice" – the beginnings of art.

Maybe a particularly effective weapon with an unusual enhancement.

The beginnings of research and development.

Many Things Tossed - Some Kept

Now we do more conscious "throw away," often sorted recycling.

An average family has a pile of packaging to toss as trash. Most of the real garbage is ground up in the disposal.

Many things our parents would have kept, repaired, repurposed, cannibalized for parts are now tossed.

In a well-to-do neighborhood of most American cities you could furnish an apartment with furniture left out to be scavenged on "trash day."

Lots of stuff goes in the throw away culture, not the things that are still worthy of status display. Things that show your class, your economic status, your fashion sense well meshed with the changing times.

Some folks over-save marginal objects and clutter-hoard, for many complex reasons.

600 as Our Special Number

The tribal clan of 600 was the magic number for human survival in Primalization – up until the beginning of the Agricultural Revolution – about 10,000 years ago.

The 600 was important because it is the right size for a human breeding group – so our genes didn't become too ingrown.

Agriculture started a slow process that at first included only a tiny percentage of humanity and progressed through hamlets to villages to towns – and about 5,000 years ago to the first cities with about 5,000 huddled humans.

5,000 People Started Cities

Ancient cities started with about 10 tribes worth of people.

Enough so the cohesion of 600 in a single tribal clan disintegrated. What would have been 150 bands and 10 tribes were now in continuous contact in one tight place, most of the time. Instead of in season- phased contact on a broad plain.

No roaming the savanna in groups of 40.

No twice a year meetings of the entire 600 of the tribal clan.

Our mental data base with space for 40 intimates and 600 in the outer circle is overwhelmed with the new 5,000.

Now "the stranger" starts and grows in numbers and in significance.

So too does "specialization."

And with specialization comes economic surplus and storage.

Then comes differentiation of "an elite" – political leaders, clergy, warriors, scribes, teachers, craft makers, traders, speculators, scientists, engineers.

The gathering hunting culture slowly begins to evaporate and disappears fast as we get closer to "our now."

Humanity has recently tipped past the point where half of us live in cities. All shoehorned into urban places.

In the United States perhaps the Cities are more critical now than the States. The United Cities of America?

With CI-ties comes CI-vilization.

Unconscious Policy

What passed for policy was habit.

The actions and reactions that produced survival were inherent in a local natural environment. With the large group of 600 people and the smaller groups of 40.

Traveling the land. Eating whatever food was available. Protecting against predators. The interweaving of the habits of daily life became "policy." All of it remembered.

Deliberated Directed Policy

Civilization changes the mixture, the tapestry of life.

The slow transition from gathering and hunting passed through agriculture. With only a few small settlements that would turn into cities there was a need for policy. Some agreement on how life should be lived.

It took about 5,000 years to get enough people together in one place to be a city. Now the need to have direction became more urgent. With different viewpoints on what should be done. Where you sit is where you stand.

You will support and defend the options that you perceive are the best and closest to you. After a time the views of individuals differ by larger amounts.

In the present we have polar opposites on most issues. Strong feelings about policy, about direction.

Yet most issues have a middle ground where the "best" negotiated solution probably lies.

There is bipolar adherence on each end of an issue. And the area for solution options are in the middle.

If many issues are involved, always in a real situation. The 3-dimensional policy options image would look like a doughnut. The prime solution options are in the doughnut hole, untouched.

A strategy is to take enough time with all the options. To eat the policy doughnut all the way through until you get to the hole.

Then when everyone has vented, and is tired, select the best option from the surviving options concentrated in the mediated middle.

Thankful

The hunter was thankful to the prey he killed. So was the entire band – thankful.

The early human recognized the sacrifice of the living animal. It allowed us, the gathering hunting band, to stay alive. Perhaps we thanked the plants we kill, as well.

Food offers us its life for our survival.

Not willingly but appreciated none-the-less by the humans.

Entitled

Food is almost an afterthought today.

It is there when we need it, and want it, in the developed world. It's in the super market or restaurant.

The hamburger is grilled, with onions, slapped on a bun, slathered with ketchup, and topped with a pickle – with never a thought to the milk-depleted dairy cow that gave its life to produce the meat. When the milk production declined to a calculated level she was butchered.

The calculation was done by a program that determines the cost of overhead for the cow, along with the mix of feed and the quality and quantity of butter fat.

Today's children delight in the hamburger and the French fries without even thinking about the cow. Or the potato. An entitlement of being in Civilization, one among so many.

117

Hard

Primalization was hard.

The body was hard.

Feet were calloused.

Life was hard.

We were ready for it.

We developed all the skills we needed to survive.

Each of us was a generalist, able to do any task.

Soft

Civilization is soft.

We have specialists all around us to do things for us.

To protect us.

To guide us.

To keep us alive.

To do the things we don't want to do.

To do the things we don't need to do, yet perhaps should. To be sharper.

The body softens, the mind softens, the emotions change.

We live a life of expectation, of entitlement, of entertainment, of undone intention.

Few want equal treatment.

Most want unearned preferred treatment.

Chapter 10 – Food – Mothering – Thanks

Practical

Our ancestors were practical – getting the job done.

Not to perfection but good enough.

There was no need for a surplus. There was no way to keep food fresh very long.

The temperature was hot and any extra food would just attract dangerous animals.

We lived day to day. Taking it as it came. Organic.

Practical.

Pampered

Civilization has become self-pampered.

Full of excesses.

Full of wants that have been converted into needs.

Racing through the non-renewable resources of the Earth for recreation, entertainment, and the search for sense-spiced novelty.

Expecting technology to right any tumbled entitlement.

The answers that come from technology are often short-thought. What can happen in the future is ignored.

Was the pampering we had in the 20th century with the automobile worth it?

We've diminished that marvelous tinker toy of chemistry, the hydrocarbon organic molecule, by burning it.

What about the air pollution with an unknown climate threshold lurking in the skies?

Is it worth it to have suburban spread across some of the most productive food growing soil?

Today's pamper may be tomorrow's privation.

Natural Immunity

During our co-evolution with the other living things on the savanna we were in a balance that maintained slow change.

Part of that balance was probably a silent truce between humans and disease-causing microbes and viruses.

Why kill the host?

Wouldn't it be better if the microbe or the virus could just stay in a human host indefinitely and not kill?

We would not come in contact with much that was new.

Other microbes and other viruses were happening in their slow-to-change niches in other species.

Better for all.

Many Allergies

With Civilization humans distort and destroy habitat for many other living things — not just for ourselves.

We have driven many large animals to extinction over the last 10,000 years,

We have also disturbed niches where microbes and viruses may have had comfy homes in other places — other species.

Now we have let them loose on us. Their regular hosts are gone - so we take on that "responsibility."

Survival is what microbe and viruses want - humans crowded in dirty cities helps.

We wind up with lots of diseases and lots of allergies. Every living thing struggles as best it can to survive.

Since we are a recent, uncertain, new host many things will kill us until we all together reach a new balance.

We became accustomed to the foods that were available to us nearby. Now the new foods from remote places need a time to stabilize in us.

Allergies are there for a reason.

Good Food

There was no way to get food from afar.

Our bodies adjusted over many years to pull nutrition from what was available.

A balanced diet was what we could get – when we could.

Pragmatic.

We ate with a bias to early morning.   Breakfast, break the fast of the night.

Grazing most of the rest of day time.

No hard-schedule meal cycle.   No need to be a disciplined factor in the production line of a factory.

A balanced diet was probably what we could get over a month's time – not every day.

Bad Food

As trade routes developed food could come from afar.

With the Industrial Revolution human habits began to mesh and blend with the needs of the food production and storage system.

Now we can eat foods that taste good. A bad test. We need food that loves us.

When food was hard to get we developed a taste for fat and sugar, sources of much energy in a small package. We were motivated to try harder to get it.

So our taste motivates us to find it and eat it. But not a lot — too hard to get.

Today fat and sugar are easy to find, on the supermarket shelves and in restaurants.

Most food is just there, all you have to do is pay a tiny fraction of your resources to be fed. But not well fed — badly fed.

You don't spend most of your day getting food.

The modern civilized diet corrodes in slow-motion. Lots of chemicals to enhance shelf-life, with unknown impact on your life.

My Motto: "Learn to love the food that loves you, that wants you to live!"

3 Full Years with Mom – Always

The first 3 years in a gathering hunting band were spent mostly with Mom – and the first year and a half probably touching skin to skin.

That gave the new member of the band a sense of what real belonging meant, a solid relationship that created the model for other connections to humans.

Close – attached – touching – connected – committed communication.

Beyond about 4 years, another baby would likely be born to your mother. The other members in the gathering hunting band had developed more interest in you. Now they would phase in to help you play your way into adulthood. And they would learn more about themselves by enabling you. Everybody wins. Everyone a student. Everyone a teacher.

3 Short Months with Mom – Maybe

A civilized baby may only have a few months with Mom.

Then its off to other care-givers. Enough to confuse the child. Who is Mom? Which one is she? Will I ride an uncertainty merry-go-round all my life?

Maybe.

The too early discontinuity with Mom probably means a more fragile set of human connection for the rest of a lifetime. So the human baby starts a cascade of indoctrination into a flawed culture.

How can you break the cycle? Do you want to break the cycle?

Since Civilized culture is unlikely to change perhaps it is best to have a child who has been nurtured in a Civilized way.

We do have to live with the actual "is."

Not the fantasy of imagined "oughts."

A Hidden – True – 6th Sense

Perhaps we did have a 6th sense of communication – brought on by real physical closeness. The brain is an electro-chemical-magnetic organ.

The magnetic force may be very tiny but perhaps detectable by related humans who lived their lives within touch distance.

Maybe brains are able to transmit and receive blurred but plausible images or emotions from close relatives.

Could the Earth's magnetic field be a carrier for human magno-chem-electronicity?

Much of what we think we know is so vague, preliminary, early, arrogant.

Too Much Communication Noise

Now we are bombarded with electro-magnetic radiation: radio, TV, GPS, WiFi, and the ever present 60 cycle hum of house current.

Plus emotional skepticism.

We call it extra-sensory-perception, ESP. Could it be magnetic sensory perception, MSP? Too much static to find out.

Not only does the electronic static create a possible interference in the human mind, there is massive implied content.

Many of the broadcast frequencies are laced with information, some may be coherent to a "tuned brain." It can happen with radio frequencies and a tooth filing.

With over 1,000,000 books published globally every year, billions of web pages, and many thousands of magazines there is an overload of knowledge accessible to a single human.

No wonder the default mode for Civilized humans is specialization. An agreed vocabulary, grouped with "common" knowledge, well-worn communication paths.

Habits that furrow the neurons of patterned thought.

Appreciative

Ancient humans appreciated the simple fact of living.

Living a life style less than poverty seen with modern eyes.

No house.

No clothes.

No refrigerator.

No car.

No formal education.

But also.

No boss.

No deadlines.

No traffic.

No mortgage.

No credit cards.

Spoiled

Modern Civilization prides itself on continuous growth.

But seems not to appreciate what it has at the moment.

Always more. Converting luxury wants into
"basic needs."

Always growth. Unsustainable.

More of everything.

An addiction to ever more.

With a cycle that seems nearly unbreakable.

Yet the Earth is finite.

Governed by biology, tectonic shifts, nature.

Not by thought-light whims of humankind.

Our human cycles are virtual, unnatural.

Nature's cycles are real, often with unknown
thresholds, with unpredictable non-linear
actions, once past any number of undiscovered
tipping points.

Chapter 11 – Space – Unified – Alert

Rounded Natural Space

Nature is rounded, very few straight lines.

There are straight lines but not many.

About the only natural straight horizontal line is the horizon, looking out at a large body of water with no shore visible on the other side. Really it's a shallow curve of the Earth, but looks straight.

The vertical straight line example would be a spider dangling from a strand of web, like a natural plumb bob.

Roundness soothes and colors the way we think.

No sharp edges.

No corners to cut. No corners to hide in.

Organic.

Bombarded with Linearity

Civilization bombards us with lines.

They are everywhere.

Architecture: ceiling tiles, floor boards, roof lines, blue prints.

Culture: line organizations, waiting in line, toe the line.

Geometry: parallel lines don't meet, usually.

Lines confront us visually and fence in the mind.

Thinking in the linear 3-dimensional box.

The linear lines of this book are an example.

127

Giving someone "a line" means a string of
language to manipulate the listener to the
advantage of the talker.

Line up and be counted.

Hunting Party

The hunting party was about 5 men – about half the men in a gathering hunting band.

It was always necessary to leave some men with the women and children to provide security.

Men had upper-body strength and did not have a specific child to care for.

They could react to any danger.

5 Person Teams

In Civilization the 5-Person Team is still
good. Basketball is an example in sports.

A project team of about 5 may still be the
most effective.

A 10s group also has lots of uses.

Parallel to the 10 adult women or the 10 adult
men in a gathering hunting band.

In sports, 9 on a baseball team, 11 on a
football team, bracketing the 10.

The 20 total adults, all the men and women, in
a gathering hunting band may be the right
figure for a modern seminar on Civilization.

The number 5 for team work has the advantage
of being odd so that agreements would be
easier to reach.

With 3 in a group there is the danger of 1 being the "odd person out."

Let It Happen

In Primalization we were reactive to the forces around us: other animals, plants, climate, geologic shifts, chance.

Let it happen.

Whatever will be will be.

Respond when it is necessary.

Don't plan.

Don't worry. Be happy.

Take it as it comes.

Make It Happen

Our urge now is to make it happen.

Force it.

Be proactive.

Plan.

Manipulate so you get what you want.

What you expect.

What you deserve.

Our generational decisions to act accumulate over the years, across the ages through the last 10,000 years, since the invention of agriculture: the Agricultural Revolution.

So we have made it happen, with profound effect on the environment, upon our many cultures, upon our selves.

We have had an unthinking prideful arrogance.
Anything we can do, we do, without much regard
to eventual consequences.

Except very lately in our history. Now we
think we can undo anything with new
technology.

We seem to think that human action can
overcome biology.

Acceptance

The default mental state was acceptance.

Take what comes, as it comes.

While the details might be a little different, the situation had
been faced, and dealt with, before.

React to the danger.

React to the hunger in the belly.

Denial

The Civilized default state of mind appears to
be denial. As individuals and as a collection
of people we often don't want to know.

And if we do know, we want to cover it over
with denial, often in layers.

It may be that the situations we face now are
too shrouded in mystery. How did we get in
this situation?

What do we do about it?

If we ignore it, maybe it will go away.

Or be overtaken by events.

Maybe an even bigger problem.

"Technology can fix anything."

Yet technology is the vehicle that often carried us into the problems we deny.

New technology enters Civilization in cascading waves, each building on the crest of the one before. Easy Cheap Oil – Gas Engine – Tractors – Cars – Paved Roads – Suburbs – Big Houses – Heating – Cooling – Global Warming – Commuting.

But now: Rarer Expensive Oil.

Unknown thresholds in non-linear feedback, and feed-forward, loops.

Very complex: much easier to deny than even try understanding.

Unified

Life was unified. We were living in the same territory for a lifetime.

The territory was perhaps as big as from Frederick, Maryland, to Fredericksburg, Virginia, along the Potomac River above and below Washington, DC. Only it was grassy savanna in Africa, not treed forest in North America.

We never left except for a survival reason, maybe into an adjacent territory to overcome a food shortage.

We were surrounded by the same animals, the same plants, the same climate, the same people – all the time. In an area we understood in finest detail. Memorized.

Only 40 people in the gathering hunting band – 24/7 – except when a group of men went hunting. They would only be gone for a few hours every few days, when prey was likely.

So we lived a unified life with little change.

We did not expect much change in: Time – Place – People –
Ideas.

Confused

In contrast: Civilization is a confusion. We
don't have a gathering hunting band to give us
stability. Our territory is usually shifting,
in motion.

We go to different parts of a city to work, to
shop, to be entertained.

We go to suburbs to sleep, to eat, to sample
our family. We are away from them most of the
time: sleeping or working or commuting or
traveling.

Our genes are usually confused. What
countries of the world did 9 generations of
ancestor parents come from? That's 1,024
people across 10 intersecting life times.

They stirred up lots of genes. The
indoctrination of Civilization creates
confusion. The culture we live in now is so
different from what our body expects.

Strangers are everywhere. We see a flood of
strangers every day in the city. We are
meeting strangers and shaking hands, touching,
perhaps the first sense to develop. Intimate
contact with a non-intimate human stranger.

We always expect, and have developed to want,
change.

An element of confusion.

Alert

While on the savanna each adult human had to be alert most of the time, "on watch", ready to sound an alarm, or become the immediate "first responder." Taking over as the capstone leader for the immediate episode.

The children at play would also develop a sense of becoming ready. Play is practice at being a full member of the band.

All the senses would be at the ready, with sight being most important, looking for disturbances, pattern recognition that could signal danger.

Seeking the unexpected.

Constant alertness with an awareness of the pacing and likelihood of adventure.

And the threat would be real. And it would be physical.

Disturbed and Stressed

Today danger can come from many directions, unexpected, abstract, continuous. Mostly "unreal." Seldom physical.

Manufactured pressure can come from jobs that have ambiguous expectations.

From deadlines that seem solid but are often arbitrary.

From relationships that are uncertain.

From trying to be "too perfect" to an uncertain specification.

Resolution of disagreements are often inconclusive and may persist for years, abstracted, tugging at the mind.

The result is a state of stress and a disturbed feeling, which can be chronic.

There is still some real physical danger: storms, earthquakes, fires, erratic traffic, crime, accidents, machine malfunctions, software malfunctions, people malfunctions.

Civilization has a much more complex profile of stress.

Much of it created by the rules of Civilization itself.

Slow Change

Our ancestors lived with horizontal change, about the same over many generations.

The nature of things for the great-grandson were unchanged from what they had been for the great-grandfather.

The innovation capacity was slight for 600 people doing about the same thing in about the same way in about the same place.

There was little motivation to find new ways when the old ways worked fine.

If it ain't broke don't fix it.

Better is the enemy of good enough.

Fast Confusing Turmoil Change

Civilization is now confronting vertical change.

A very steep slope of constant change.

Each day is a new technological day, new processes, new inventions, new fashions all in flux.

Our genes expect horizontal change that takes a long time to creep up.

Our culture gives us change that explodes straight up! No wonder we are stressed!

Our DNA longs for stability. Our Civilization demands change. A recipe for human emotions boiling in a pressure-cookered mind.

Roger Gilbertson

Chapter 12 – Adult – Life – Brain

Play to Become an Adult

Children are adults who haven't grown up enough to have many experiences. Play is a low risk way of practicing to be an adult.

After 21 years of playing at being an adult you became a beginner adult. You had reached your full physical growth. Your mind had spent 21 years memorizing the environment you lived within.

Play to Remain a Child

Now a lot of play, a lot of entertainment, a lot of recreation seems aimed at remaining a child, unable to take on, or face, full adult responsibility.

Continuously seeking another novelty, for the sake of novelty, self-fulfilling.

We go to movies. We watch sports. We read novels. Trying to get a grip on what's happening. We can feel a sense of understanding our small local area, but wider areas are much harder.

No one has the wider answers, only personal speculations, usually about the self and local lifescape.

The overload of Civilization is too much.

We never mature enough now to truly know what we are doing.

We do the best we can with the sampling we know. Which might improve with the wisdom that comes with aging.

So we wing it.

Absolutes are rare, probabilities, common.

"The truth" is hard to come by. Real 100% chance is elusive.

"A guessed truth" is easy, a simulated 100% chance with belief at its heart.

There isn't anyone out there who "knows the real truth" - only other estimators, other speculators.

21 Years to Adulthood

It took a full 21 years to reach the age of maturity.

The time was needed for both physical and mental growth.

The body grew. The brain grew.

The brain gathered knowledge to become a mind.

The baby turned toddler. The toddler became a child. The child became a teen. The teen became an adult.

It took that long to get the body and the mind together to be a full scale human.

Technology Prevents Maturity

As technology continued its expansion, from simple tools to the full technology bubble we live in today, it takes longer to reach true adulthood.

Physically we still become mature at 21.

The mental demands of an ever more complex Civilization increases the years to reach maturity in crafted mind content.

It may now take more years to mature, to carry the load of change every day, than we have years in a human life.

We may never mature, always a child.

We don't know enough at 21 to really be fully functional as Civilized adults.

Maybe we know enough at 42.

Maybe not. Yet we still function.

Life Accepting

The members of a gathering band knew the cycles of life.

They expected to die whenever it was their time to go.

Death was a part of life.

Life was about the same when they were old as it was when they were young.

They had seen a lot when they became an elder.

Their wisdom was prized because of repeated experience.

When they left it was probably with peaceful expectation.

And with little mourning for such a natural happening.

Fighting Off Death

Now we live with constant novelty.

There is something new just over the horizon.

Life at any age is fun.

Tomorrow will be different.

Novelty surrounds us, calls us.

We fight death, expect, and want, to live to
an old age.

Denial of death seems a very reasonable
concept for the fully Civilized.

It seems unnatural to leave such an
interesting, ever changing, existence.

100% Brain

The brain of "the wild" is the normal – 100% brain.

Primalization was a form of wild.

We needed a full brain.

We developed a bigger, more complex, physical brain over 2,500,000 years.

75% Brain

Experiments with a wild fox species in Russia
showed that taming them decreased their brain
by 10%. That was across about 20 generations.
May not apply to humans, but then it might.

Other longer term examples of domestication
among animals show up to a 25% decrease in
brain size. Maybe in brain function.

Civilization is a form of taming.

Brain size isn't everything, some
effectiveness lies in structure.

We often just don't know what we are doing to
brain function and thought and action.

Chapter 13 – Commons – Full – Finagle

Natural Commons

Before we became awkward with the planet, everything was "Commons."

We lived in a territory that was big enough for our 600 humans to roam around. We all "owned" it.

We could gather plants. Hunt animals. Eat and drink and poop and wander wherever we wanted.

The environment was huge compared to us and could respond to anything we did to it easily. We were just another animal in the prey and predator cycle. Co-evolving as we passed through millions of years of development.

Technical Commons

Now it is different. New "Commons" are being created all the time, seams in Civilization.

Every emerging technology starts a new opening door for humans to enter and use.

Territory in these abstract commons is staked out with patents, trademarks, copyrights – and proprietary secrets. Usually with the profit imperative as the driving force.

Dollar-intensive energy is quick to develop and often impacts a few people who, through guided-chance, are near by. With dollar-luck to match, there may be large profits to be made and accumulated.

The cost to the larger group of humans comes later – and can be big, but difficult to prove.

141

By the time large numbers of dollars have been gathered some can be used to support an effective network of manipulation, to maintain access to scarce material and dangerous markets.

A supersized entity with supersized resources can easily cast "reasonable" doubt on contrary evidence that might shrink it.

Plausible deniability is often a critical policy element.

The lately discovered unanticipated cost of earlier damage, and the future toll of continued use, is seldom re-paid by the triggering people. Hard to prove across time. Financial meltdowns. Environmental disasters. Deniable.

Along comes the next technical commons to jump into, and capture the next human load of attention.

Full Spectrum Thought

The gatherer-hunter had to be a full thinker, all the time.

The survival "job" depended on being able to respond to any crisis – any event.

Bare life for our ancestors was simple. Yet the thinking could be complex at times and had to be very rapid.

Using all possible solutions along a spectrum.

Binary Thought

Today we are in a technology explosion!

And we are doing it with 7,000,000,000 other people, all now potentially connected.

Each with a set of incremental speculations on what a culture is, what life is about, what should be done next.

It is too complex to understand in full, so the fallback, default position is: simplify.

The way you do that is select a few issues and a few facts as evidence.

That is the recipe for binary thinking.

Even thought the most likely solution, or option, or decision, is in the middle. Often the edges of the policy space get supported by committed advocates.

Simple cause and effect is rare. Causes and effects are more likely, many causes, many effects.

Shorthanded binary thinking becomes the default for individuals and organizations.

The policy map is usually a large sphere with many factions, many points of view. Some mutually supporting in part, others in partial opposition.

Seldom neat. Seldom clean. Always extended past deadlines.

Unpleasantly non-binary.

Co-Evolution Contentment

We were content developing with all other life on Earth.

We were reactive to the changes around us, mostly in slow motion. With some occasional rapid emergencies that we met and solved quickly. Then went back to taking it as it came. It was dangerous, sometimes deadly, yet we survived.

Co-Experiment Intensive

So here we are in a huge human experiment with all the living things on the planet.

With no control group.

Are we the 6th Extinction? There have been 5 major extinctions before us. There have been many species on Earth now gone.

We exist in a paradox – trying to be Civilized in culture while living in a Primalized body in biology.

How do we find that personal balance point that gets us through a fulfilled life?

All individual lives end. Species come to an end, too.

We would prefer a longer run.

As individuals and as a species.

Grab life with both hands, both sides of the brain, all senses!

Find a compromise, a negotiation, to give you some freedom in this caged world.

Be optimistic if you can.

Pretend optimism if you must, and it will "take."

Your human life is a grand adventure!

Fight – Fight – or Finagle

We learned to fight or flight in the jungle, before we began to surf the east side of the Great Rift. Because of the dense vegetation, short sight distances, rapid instant reaction was needed.

Instant fight or instant flight.

As the trees left us, and we started walking on our lengthening legs, we used our long-range, binocular color vision to find our way through a dangerous savanna.

We added finagle to our bundle of skills. We had more time to think, a few seconds, maybe more.

We now had a 3rd choice. Now we had time to bluff, or find another blended choice for action. Not just Fight or Flight.

Fight – Flight – Finagle!

We had a middle ground, a place for mixed tactic, or even a new approach.

We have been finagling other animals for many years.

Bluff Mostly

In Civilization we bluff a lot of the time. We manipulate other humans and situations. Not many animals around to bluff any more.

We want others to do what we want and think as we do. Controlling what others think.

It doesn't normally happen that way, others with the same thoughts. But we don't know, can't mind read.

So we bluff. We manipulate. We negotiate. We try to fit in.

Bluffing is how many pinnacle leaders get there. Bluffing while they become really good at a specialty. Then find themselves unable to deal with real long-range issues that need broad policy.

About more general situations.

About how a covey of specialists fit together to perform a mission in a quicksand culture. Some bluffing becomes a part of leadership finagle.

First performed by the maturing leader and later, with better financing, by a public relations staff with media savvy.

Civilization at its core may be the result of a 10,000-year, elongated, elegant, elaborate, maxi-finagle.

Chapter 14 – Thanks for Reading!

Conclusion: It's been a mostly happy life!

It's been fun to have a lifetime mission and be able to follow through with it! Auditioning specialties, becoming partly a generalist.

Thanks for looking over my shoulder!

My writing has been mostly to better understand myself.

It may be interesting or useful to others.

Maybe you? I hope so.

I don't really have a nuanced marketing plan. I'll probably dance around some with self-publishing this book. Or do a close substitute: allow for print-on-demand for the physical molecular book. With ebooks available in some formats.

Many of my professional speaker friends do self-publishing.

They are experts who talk, and write.

Me too!

I like to talk to audiences and write!

Ask me to give a speech to your group.

The Web Is Out There

I know – I know.

The Web is out there. Busily chomping on content, not sure how it's going to self-define as technology gallops forward.

The Web is a new commons where many can exploit fresh freedoms. Others see the Web through different minds.

I've had a website for over a decade.

I remember using early, tentative versions of what became the Web in the dim depths of the 1960s, long before commercialization.

I still prefer to talk to living people, eye-to-eye, in the same room, in the same space, breathing the same air, touchable.

The Web creates hunger for real human contact.

A golden age for the public speaker may be fast approaching.

Folks will lust for more human contact, Internet backlash.

"The mBook" Is Still Out There

The book, I love books! The mbook is an identifiable physical object, made of molecules. You can pick it up when you want.

Take it anywhere. Read it wherever there is light. Don't need any electricity to use it. Lincoln's firelight reading.

Give it to a friend with your notes in it. Donate it to a thrift shop when you don't need it. Let it wander to a new home.

But mostly, a book is not just a collection of easily clicked away electrons, activating a monitor, in competition with other electrons shrieking for priority: emails, a calendar alert, hyper-linked "now" events.

Breakers of attention. Preventers of focus. Electronic isolation.

A book creates within a dedicated time: your rapt attention.

Molecules at rest for the life of the book and its ideas.

To you, Reader!

From this writer.

Thank You for Surfing Among my Words!

Appendix

Some Resources

These are some of the books that have helped shape my multi-spectrum world views.

Allport, G. W.   On becoming: Basic considerations for a psychology of personality. New Haven, CN: Yale University Press, 1955.

Bach, G. R., & Goldberg, H. Creative aggression. New York, NY: Avon, 1974.

Bloom, A. (Ed. and Trans.). The 'Republic' of Plato. New York: Basic Books, 1968.

Bolles, R. N. The three boxes of life. Berkeley, CA: Ten Speed Press, 1978.

Bronowski, J. The ascent of man. Boston: Little, Brown and Company, 1973.

Camus, Albert. The rebel. New York: Vintage Books, 1960.

Cox, H. The secular city. New York: Macmillan, 1965.

Cummings, D. W. & Herum, J.   Tempo: Life, work and leisure.   Boston: Houughton Mifflin, 1974.

Curtis, C. P., & Greenslet, F.   (Ed.).   The practical cogitator or the thinker's anthology. Boston: Houghton Mifflin, 1962.

Dawkins, R. The selfish gene. London: Paladin, 1976.

Doxiadis, C. (Ed.).   Anthropopolis: city for human development.   New York: W.W. Norton, 1974.

Durant, W. The story of philosophy. Garden City, NY: Garden City Publishing, 1943.

Erikson, E. H. Identity: Youth and crisis. New York: W.W. Norton, 1968.

Fletcher, J. F. Situation ethics. Philadelphia: Westminster Press, 1966.

Fuller, Buckminster. Operating manual for spaceship earth. New York: Simon and Schuster, 1969.

Gardner, Howard. Frames of mind. New York: Basic Books, 1983.

Gardner, J.W. Excellence. New York: Harper & Row, 1961.

Gleick, J. Chaos: Making a new science. New York: Viking, 1987.

Hall, E. T. The hidden dimension. Garden City, NY: Anchor Press, 1966.

Hampden-Turner, C. Maps of the mind. New York: Macmillan, 1981.

Hardin, Garrett. The Tragedy of the Commons. Science 13 December 1968.

Hayakawa, S.I. Language in thought and action. New York: Harcourt, Brace and World, 1964.

Heilbroner, R. L. The worldly philosophers. New York: Simon & Schuster, 1961.

Herodotus. The histories. Baltimore: Penguin, 1954.

Hennessey, J., & Papanek, V. Nomadic furniture. New York: Pantheon, 1973.

Hoffer, E. The true believer. New York: Mentor, 1951.

Hofstadter, Douglas R. Godel, Escher, Bach: An Eternal Golden Braid. New York: Basic Books, 1979.

Hume, D. An inquiry concerning human understanding. Indianapolis: Bobbs-Merrill, 1955.

Jacobs, Jane. The death and life of great American cities. New York: Random House, 1961.

Jay, A. Corporation man. New York: Random House, 1971.

Jourard, S. M. The transparent self. New York: D. Van Nostrand, 1971.

Jung, C. G. Man and his symbols. New York: Dell, 1964.

Kennedy, Paul. The rise and fall of the great powers: Economic change and military conflict from 1500 to 2000. New York: Random House, 1987.

Koberg, D. & Bagnall, J. The universal traveler: A soft- systems guide to creativity, problem-solving, and the process of design. Los Altos, CA: William Kaufmann, 1974.

Kuhn, Thomas S. The structure of scientific revolutions. Chicago: University of Chicago Press, 1970.

Lakoff, G., & Johnson, M. Metaphors we live by. Chicago: University of Chicago Press, 1980.

Lapp, R. E. The logarithmic century: Charting future shock. Englewood Cliffs, NJ: Prentice-Hall, 1973.

Leakey, R., & Lewin, R. People of the lake: Mankind and its beginnings. New York: Anchor Press/Doubleday, 1978.

Leontief, W. The future of the world economy. New York: Oxford University Press, 1977.

Machiavelli, N. The prince. New York: Bantam, 1966.

Mair, L. Primitive government. Baltimore: Penguin, 1964.

Maslow, A. H. The further reaches of human nature. San Francisco: Esalen, 1970.

May, R. The courage to create. New York: Bantam, 1975.

Meadows, D.H.; Meadows, D.L.; Randers, J.; and Behrens, W.W. The limits to growth. New York: Signet, 1972.

Miller, G. A. The magical number seven, plus or minus two. The Psychological Review, March 1956.

Morris, D. The naked ape. New York: McGraw-Hill, 1967.

Naisbitt, J. Megatrends. New York: Warner Books, 1982.

Orwell, G. 1984. New York: New American Library, 1949.

Peck, M. S. The different drum. New York: Simon and Schuster, 1987.

Peters, T.J. and Waterman, R.H. In search of excellence. New York: Harper and Row, 1982.

Pfeiffer, John E. The creative explosion: An inquiry into the origins of art and religion. NYC: Harper and Row, 1982.

Pirsig, R. Zen and the art of motorcycle maintenance. New York: Morrow, 1979.

Progoff, I. At a journal workshop. New York: Dialogue House Library, 1975.

Rifkin, J. Time wars: The primary conflict in human history. New York: Henry Holt & Co., Inc., 1987.

Sagan, C. The dragons of Eden. New York: Random House, 1977.

Sale, K. Human scale. New York: Coward, McCann and Geoghegan, 1980.

Schumacher, E. Small is beautiful. New York: Harper and Row, 1973.

Smith, A. The wealth of nations. New York: Penguin Classics, 1776.

Stevens, A. Archetypes: A natural history of the self. New York: William Morrow and Company, Inc., 1982.

Taylor, F. The principles of scientific management. New York: 1911.

Thayer, F. An end to hierarchy and competition: administration in the post-affluent world. New York: Franklin Watts, 1981.

Thoreau, H.D. Walden and On the duty of civil disobedience. New York: Rinehart, 1948.

Thurow, L. The zero-sum society. New York: Basic Books, 1980.

Tiger, L. Optimism: The biology of hope. New York: Simon and Schuster, 1979.

Toffler, A. Future Shock. New York: Bantam, 1970.

Toynbee, Arnold. A study of history. New York: Oxford University Press, 1946.

Turner, F. J. The frontier in American history. New York: 1920.

Tzu, Sun. The art of war. London: Oxford Press, 1963.

Veblen, Thorstein. The theory of the leisure class. New York: MacMillan, 1899.

Viscott, D. Feel free. New York: Dell, 1971.

Wiener, Norbert. Cybernetics. Cambridge, MA: MIT Press, 1961.

Winston, P. H. Artificial intelligence. Reading, MA: Addison-Wesley, 1984.

Internet & World Wide Web

The Internet is another rich resource. Here are some blog feeds:

Betsy Lerner
http://betsylerner.wordpress.com/feed/

Brain Pickings
http://feeds.feedburner.com/brainpickings/rss

Cosmic Variance
http://cosmicvariance.com/feed/

Dot Earth
http://dotearth.blogs.nytimes.com/feed/

Freedom to Learn
http://www.psychologytoday.com/blog/freedom-learn/feed

InfoGraphics
http://visual.ly/top_rss.xml

Information Is Beautiful
http://feeds.feedburner.com/InformationIsBeautiful

Scientific American – Mind & Brain
http://rss.sciam.com/sciam/mind-and-brain

Roger Gilbertson

Seth Blog
http://feeds.feedburner.com/typepad/sethsmainblog

storytelling with data
http://feeds.feedburner.com/StorytellingWithData

Visualizing Economics
http://feeds.feedburner.com/VisualizingEconomics

zen habits
http://feeds.feedburner.com/zenhabits

.

Glossary

Civilization

The cultural environment for humans that very slowly spread across the globe from a tiny core of specialization triggered by agriculture perhaps 10,000 years ago. Creeping along from only a few cities 5,000 years ago, humanity is now in high speed acceleration with more than 50% of us in urban places.

eCulture

Electronic culture is based on a heavy use of communications based on electronics, particularly micro-electronics. Pace is fast. Messages are passed quickly and easily forgotten. An example of an artifact is the eBook. It is a virtual object and exists only as a sparked pixel on a screen. It has no physical presence as an object.

mCulture

Molecular culture is based on molecules that are present in a physical state. Objects and transmission are real. An example is an mBook. A molecular book which exists and can be easily read anywhere and moved and traded. It can have a long life.

Gathering Hunting Band

An ancient group of humans. Gathering is first because the gathering function provided most of the regular food. If food was hard to get the hunting function could provide a safety net. There were about 10 women, 10 men, and 20 children in a band.

Gathering Hunting Tribal-Clan

About 15 gathering hunting bands were in a tribal-clan. The territory was about 1000 square miles. The clan would get together about every 6 months for a few weeks of being in close proximity based on food at changes of the season. The clan of about 600 was the only human presence known to its members. Any other human-like group would be remote. There were about 150 women, 150 men, and 300 children in the tribe.

Human Swarm

A human swarm is a group of modern humans using high technology communications. This can include newspapers, books, the telegraph, telephone, radio, television, cell phones, and now the Internet across the World Wide Web. At its highest-level the swarm will soon include all of civilized humankind alive on the globe at the moment.

Smaller swarms include groups who do modern forms of "gathering and hunting" for a specialized purpose. Examples would be the corporate swarms who gathers for profit and the country swarms which gather for reasons of history, politics, and power.

Primalization

The human condition that existed as the lead-in to civilization. Primalization began being displaced by civilization about 10,000 years ago. The most recent era of Primalization was lived in a gathering and hunting tribal-clan life style.

Primal metaphor

"Primal" is the original, fundamental, first. "Metaphor" is something that does not literally apply but suggests a resemblance. The two together have a special meaning here. Primal applies to the 5,000,000 years of human life before the Current Era. Metaphor is used to provide contrast of human characteristics developed during that long period with the cultural characteristics of Civilization.

What happened to our 250,000 generations of ancestors still has a strong inertia through a mix of genes, memes, and collective unconscious which may persist in all of us. The 500 generations since the agricultural revolution started and the 20 generations since the onset of the industrial revolution pale in comparison.

Concept Index

Questions

1. Who are the 40 people in your life that are like a gathering hunting band? Your first or inner circle.

2. Who are some of the 600 people in your modern gathering hunting tribal-clan? Your second circle.

3. Who are some of the folks you now that are nearly strangers?

4. What are the differences you feel in your life texture that are unlike the way you might have lived as a gatherer hunter?

Contact - Connection

<u>A Free-Range Human in a Caged World</u> is available as a physical book from Amazon, plus other places if it gains readers.

Want a Talk, a Conversation, or Coaching, or Consulting?

Want a Speculation on Your Group's Primal Story?

Want a Speech! I'm good at them!

To a Band of 40. To a Tribal-Clan of 600. Whatever numbers. Any size audience. How did a group of Civilized humans get to today, from Primalization? What insights pop?

How can a modern culture mesh with wisdom from ancient ancestors? Want your group to have insight speculations? Explore the Idea.

Write a physical letter:

> Roger Gilbertson
> Box 103
> Washington, DC   20044-0103

Even Better Send Email: <u>Gilbertson@gmail.com</u>

There are highlights about any Civilized situation, seen through the filtering eyes of Primalization. Any modern gathering band can navigate through virtual time for some Lessons Learned.

What's going on with: the people – the place – the things – intentions – goals – vision – mission – results?

I'm a fast dancer on my verbal feet. Usually funny.

Idea stimulation from an exuberant extroverted elder!

Trading resources depends on time, place, people.

If you like the book tell your friends - write a review.

If you don't like the book tell your enemies.

Epilogue Acknowledgments

My life owes much to many.

To the Norwegian farmers and Vikings, my ancient ancestors.

To Myrtle Julianna Gunderson and George H. Gilbertson my parents with grandparent wisdom.

To my brother Warren and my sister Beverly.

To my wife Meg.

To my children Gambi and Erik and their mother, Marilyn.

To my son-in-law Moe and grandson Corbin.

To the Gilbertson, Gunderson, Hoffman, DeWolf, Benesch extended families.

To the modern gathering hunting bands in my life:

Tuesday Evening Elders, Veteran Speakers Retreat, Colorado 1960s SigEp Reunion, fraternity brothers, friends, neighbors, Credit Union volunteers, Navy shipmates, Mensa folks, Team America, classmates, the Orwellians, alumni associate members, many library and book store staffs, business colleagues, people across a wide variety of fields, strangers after random conversations, authors, specialists, and others.

To all the members of our shared human species, confronting mortality, while embedded in an infinite, timeless cosmos.

We have been about 110,000,000,000 so far. With about 7,000,000,000 sharing the Earth and alive today.

Everyone contributes to the network that is you, me, us.

Thanks, with acknowledgment to all!

Hurray, humans!

About the Author

Roger Gilbertson had an adventurous **Dad** who **auditioned specialties**. Roger's story is about doing different things.

That's his story for a lifetime. Trying one thing after another, a multi-specialist, a **proactive generalist**, by design.

He's done that with callings, careers, geography, education, recreation – and groups of people. In trying to understand his generalist impulse, he studied the long background of us humans.

Back to basics – ancient fundamentals. Living in bands. Our genetic legacy. Our cultural heritage. **Primalization.**

From his **Mother** – Roger got the support and nurturance a Primalization baby had. Setting the course to navigate his **relationship with Civilization**.

Over many years Roger has auditioned careers in **business, non-profits, consulting, the Navy, Federal Government, teaching, public speaking, and writing.** Along the path he **worked in the White House** and **ran for Congress.** He **retired as a Rear Admiral** in the United States Navy Reserve.

In schools he studied math, engineering, science, physics, English, sociology, philosophy, law, psychology, business, anthropology, economics, accounting, leadership, history. From the **Baltimore Polytechnic** Institute High School to a doctorate from the **University of Southern California** – with lots of learning ports of call on the way.

Formal education tries by indoctrination to give you what Civilization wants you to know. **Experience education** tells what you really need, by doing, and gives **honest 'lessons learned'.**

Writings give the frozen thoughts of an author at the time of printing.

You are reading an example now.

A Free-Range Human
in a *Caged World*

From Primalization
into Civilization

Roger Gilbertson

A Finagle Watcher Book

First Edition

Made in the USA
Charleston, SC
13 August 2013